U.S. PET OWNERSHIP & DEMOGRAPHICS SOURCEBOOK

**Center for Information Management
American Veterinary Medical Association**

U.S. PET OWNERSHIP & DEMOGRAPHICS SOURCEBOOK

Copyright © 1993 by the American Veterinary Medical Association
Library of Congress Catalog Card Number: 92-74456
ISBN 1-882691-00-8

Reproduction or transmission in any form, electronic or mechanical, including photocopying, microfilming, and recording, or by any information storage or retrieval system, in whole or in part, is prohibited without written permission by the American Veterinary Medical Association.

Additional copies of this report may be purchased from:

Center for Information Management
American Veterinary Medical Association
1931 North Meacham Road, Suite 100
Schaumburg, Illinois 60173
708-925-8070 Ext. 297

Preface

Pets are important to American society. In fact, nearly 55 million households in the United States have a dog, cat, bird, or other companion animal as a member of their family. Pets are popular because they provide companionship, joy, unconditional love, a sense of safety, and, often, service.

U.S. Pet Ownership and Demographics Sourcebook summarizes statistical data about household ownership and demographics of pets, expenditures for pet food, use of and expenditures for veterinary medical services, data on registration of dog and cat breeds, and the population and distribution of veterinary medical professionals. Also, simple formulas, derived from ownership statistics, are provided to assist in the estimation of the population of pets in a community or local area.

Statistics reported here are, in large part, the result of a national survey conducted by the American Veterinary Medical Association. Survey forms were sent to 80,000 randomly selected households. Nearly 56,000 individuals, almost 70%, were kind enough to participate in the survey project.

The report is divided into six chapters: population of pets, breeds of pets, demographics of pet ownership, profiles of pet-owning households, expenditures for pet food and veterinary services, and the veterinary medical profession. Appendices provide information about study methodology and statistical inference and organizational resources for further information. A final section on formulas provides readers with the means to estimate the number of pet-owning households or the size of the pet population in a community.

Statistical research was conducted by the Center for Information Management, a not-for-profit research and database management department of the American Veterinary Medical Association.

U.S. Pet Demographic and Ownership Sourcebook is one element of the Center for Information Management's strategy to develop and integrate the best information possible on the companion animal population and the market for companion animal services.

The completion of the research and publication of this report required the commitment and support of many individuals.

Thanks are due the Executive Board, management, and staff of the American Veterinary Medical Association for their confidence in and support of the Center for Information Management.

A special thank you is given to Kurt Matushek, D.V.M., Publications Division, for editing the report, and to Michael Walters, Public Information Division, for thoughtful ideas and encouragement.

I am especially grateful to three individuals in the AVMA Center for Information Management: Jih-Jing Yang, Ph.D., Research Analyst, who programmed, compiled, and analyzed the statistical findings; Deborah J. Binder, Research Assistant, who drafted the text, compiled the index, and managed the entire report in desk-top publishing; and Dana C. Bucalo, Research Assistant, who assisted in the preparation of tables and figures.

We are also grateful to Mr. Tom Dent from the Cat Fanciers' Association and Mr. John Mandeville from The American Kennel Club who enthusiastically provided historical breed registration data.

Thanks are given to veterinarians, other pet care professionals, pet owners, and pet enthusiasts, who have supported and encouraged the continued investment in quality research and meaningful databases on pet ownership and demographics.

In dedication to Kitty, Susie Q, Mimi, and Lucky.

J. Karl Wise, Ph.D.
Director of Information Management

Table of Contents

CHAPTER 1   POPULATION OF PETS — 1
- PET OWNERSHIP — 1
- DOG OWNERSHIP — 6
- CAT OWNERSHIP — 11
- BIRD OWNERSHIP — 16
- HORSE OWNERSHIP — 20
- OTHER PET OWNERSHIP — 24

CHAPTER 2   BREEDS OF PETS — 27
- DOG BREEDS — 27
- CAT BREEDS — 32

CHAPTER 3   DEMOGRAPHICS OF PET OWNERSHIP — 35
- PET OWNERSHIP DEMOGRAPHICS — 35
- DOG OWNERSHIP DEMOGRAPHICS — 39
- CAT OWNERSHIP DEMOGRAPHICS — 43
- BIRD OWNERSHIP DEMOGRAPHICS — 47
- HORSE OWNERSHIP DEMOGRAPHICS — 51

CHAPTER 4   PROFILES OF PET-OWNING HOUSEHOLDS — 55
- PROFILES OF PET-OWNING HOUSEHOLDS — 55
- PROFILES OF DOG-OWNING HOUSEHOLDS — 62
- PROFILES OF CAT-OWNING HOUSEHOLDS — 66
- PROFILES OF BIRD-OWNING HOUSEHOLDS — 70
- PROFILES OF HORSE-OWNING HOUSEHOLDS — 74

CHAPTER 5 PET FOOD AND VETERINARY SERVICES FOR PETS — 79

- PET CARE — 79
- PET FOOD EXPENDITURES — 81
- DOG VETERINARY SERVICES AND EXPENDITURES — 82
- CAT VETERINARY SERVICES AND EXPENDITURES — 87
- BIRD VETERINARY SERVICES AND EXPENDITURES — 91
- HORSE VETERINARY SERVICES AND EXPENDITURES — 94
- OTHER PET VETERINARY SERVICES AND EXPENDITURES — 97

CHAPTER 6 VETERINARY MEDICAL PROFESSION — 99

- VETERINARY MEDICINE — 99
- AMERICAN VETERINARY MEDICAL ASSOCIATION — 99
- NATION — 99
- STATE — 101
- GENDER — 105
- AGE — 106
- PRIMARY EMPLOYMENT — 108
- VETERINARY MEDICAL COLLEGE — 112
- YEAR OF GRADUATION — 114

APPENDIX A STUDY METHODOLOGY — 117

- SURVEY — 117
- SAMPLE REPRESENTATIVENESS — 120
- STATISTICAL INFERENCE — 124

APPENDIX B RESOURCES — 125

FORMULAS — 126

List of Tables

Chapter 1	**Population of Pets**	1
Table 1-1.	Pet Ownership and Population Estimates, 1987, 1991	3
Table 1-2.	Percentage of Pet Owners That Owned Another Pet, 1991	5
Table 1-3.	Dog Ownership, by State, 1991	7
Table 1-4.	Number of Dogs Owned by Households, 1983, 1987, 1991	9
Table 1-5.	Percentage of Dogs Owned by Age of Dog, 1983, 1987, 1991	10
Table 1-6.	Cat Ownership, by State, 1991	12
Table 1-7.	Number of Cats Owned by Households, 1983, 1987, 1991	14
Table 1-8.	Percentage of Cats Owned by Age of Cat, 1983, 1987, 1991	15
Table 1-9.	Bird Ownership, by Region, 1991	16
Table 1-10.	Number of Birds Owned by Households, 1987, 1991	17
Table 1-11.	Percentage of Birds Owned by Age of Bird, 1987, 1991	18
Table 1-12.	Horse Ownership, by Region, 1991	20
Table 1-13.	Number of Horses Owned by Households, 1987, 1991	21
Table 1-14.	Percentage of Horses Owned by Age of Horse, 1983, 1987, 1991	22
Table 1-15.	Percentage of Households That Owned Other Pets, 1983, 1987, 1991	24
Table 1-16.	Other Pet Ownership, 1991	25
Chapter 2	**Breeds of Pets**	27
Table 2-1.	Dogs Registered by the American Kennel Club Inc., 1982, 1992	28
Table 2-2.	Cats Registered by Cat Fanciers' Association, 1982, 1992	33
Chapter 3	**Pet Demographics**	35
Table 3-1.	Demographics of Pet Ownership, by Life-stage, 1991	36
Table 3-2.	Demographics of Pet Ownership, by Household Income, 1991	37
Table 3-3.	Demographics of Pet Ownership, by Household Size, 1991	37
Table 3-4.	Demographics of Pet Ownership, by Home Ownership, 1991	38
Table 3-5.	Demographics of Dog Ownership, by Life-stage, 1991	39
Table 3-6.	Demographics of Dog Ownership, by Household Income, 1991	40
Table 3-7.	Demographics of Dog Ownership, by Household Size, 1991	41
Table 3-8.	Demographics of Dog Ownership, by Home Ownership, 1991	42
Table 3-9.	Demographics of Cat Ownership, by Life-stage, 1991	43

Table 3-10.	Demographics of Cat Ownership, by Household Income, 1991	44
Table 3-11.	Demographics of Cat Ownership, by Household Size, 1991	45
Table 3-12.	Demographics of Cat Ownership, by Home Ownership, 1991	46
Table 3-13.	Demographics of Bird Ownership, by Life-stage, 1991	47
Table 3-14.	Demographics of Bird Ownership, by Household Income, 1991	48
Table 3-15.	Demographics of Bird Ownership, by Household Size, 1991	49
Table 3-16.	Demographics of Bird Ownership, by Home Ownership, 1991	50
Table 3-17.	Demographics of Horse Ownership, by Life-stage, 1991	51
Table 3-18.	Demographics of Horse Ownership, by Household Income, 1991	52
Table 3-19.	Demographics of Horse Ownership, by Household Size, 1991	53
Table 3-20.	Demographics of Horse Ownership, by Home Ownership, 1991	54
Chapter 4	**Profiles of Pet-Owning Households**	**55**
Table 4-1.	Profile of Pet-Owning Households, by Life-stage, 1991	56
Table 4-2.	Profile of Pet-Owning Households, by Household Income, 1991	57
Table 4-3.	Profile of Pet-Owning Households, by Household Size, 1991	58
Table 4-4.	Profile of Pet-Owning Households, by Home Ownership, 1991	59
Table 4-5.	Profile of Pet-Owning Households, by Type of Residence, 1991	59
Table 4-6.	Profile of Pet-Owning Households, by Population Density, 1991	60
Table 4-7.	Profile of Pet-Owning Households, by Male Head Education, 1991	60
Table 4-8.	Profile of Pet-Owning Households, by Female Head Education, 1991	61
Table 4-9.	Profile of Dog-Owning Households, by Life-stage, 1991	62
Table 4-10.	Profile of Dog-Owning Households, by Household Income, 1991	64
Table 4-11.	Profile of Dog-Owning Households, by Household Size, 1991	64
Table 4-12.	Profile of Dog-Owning Households, by Home Ownership, 1991	65
Table 4-13.	Profile of Cat-Owning Households, by Life-stage, 1991	66
Table 4-14.	Profile of Cat-Owning Households, by Household Income, 1991	67
Table 4-15.	Profile of Cat-Owning Households, by Household Size, 1991	68
Table 4-16.	Profile of Cat-Owning Households, by Home Ownership, 1991	69
Table 4-17.	Profile of Bird-Owning Households, by Life-stage, 1991	70
Table 4-18.	Profile of Bird-Owning Households, by Household Income, 1991	71
Table 4-19.	Profile of Bird-Owning Households, by Household Size, 1991	72
Table 4-20.	Profile of Bird-Owning Households, by Home Ownership, 1991	73
Table 4-21.	Profile of Horse-Owning Households, by Life-stage, 1991	74
Table 4-22.	Profile of Horse-Owning Households, by Household Income, 1991	75

Table 4-23.	Profile of Horse-Owning Households, by Household Size, 1991	76
Table 4-24.	Profile of Horse-Owning Households, by Home Ownership, 1991	77
Chapter 5	**Pet Food and Veterinary Services for Pets**	**79**
Table 5-1.	Age and Gender of Person Responsible for Pet Care, 1991	79
Table 5-2.	Expenditures for Dog Food, 1991	81
Table 5-3.	Expenditures for Cat Food, 1991	81
Table 5-4.	Expenditures for Bird Food, 1991	81
Table 5-5.	Expenditures for Horse Food, 1991	81
Table 5-6.	Dog-Owning Households That Currently Have a Veterinarian for Their Dogs, 1987, 1991	82
Table 5-7.	Services & Products for Dogs Provided at Most Recent Veterinary Visit, 1987, 1991	83
Table 5-8.	Veterinary Visits, for Dogs, per Year, 1983, 1987, 1991	84
Table 5-9.	Veterinary Expenditures, for Dogs, per Year, 1983, 1987, 1991	85
Table 5-10.	Cat-Owning Households That Currently Have a Veterinarian for Their Cats, 1987, 1991	87
Table 5-11.	Services & Products for Cats Provided at Most Recent Veterinary Visit for Cats, 1987, 1991	88
Table 5-12.	Veterinary Visits, for Cats, per Year, 1983, 1987, 1991	89
Table 5-13.	Veterinary Expenditures, for Cats, per Year, 1983, 1987, 1991	90
Table 5-14.	Bird-Owning Households That Currently Have a Veterinarian for Their Birds, 1987, 1991	91
Table 5-15.	Services & Products for Birds Provided at Most Recent Veterinary Visit, 1987, 1991	92
Table 5-16.	Veterinary Visits, for Birds, per Year, 1991	93
Table 5-17.	Veterinary Expenditures, for Birds, per Year, 1987, 1991	93
Table 5-18.	Horse-Owning Households That Currently Have a Veterinarian for Their Horses, 1987, 1991	94
Table 5-19.	Services & Products for Horses Provided at Most Recent Veterinary Visit, 1987, 1991	94
Table 5-20.	Veterinary Visits, for Horses, per Year, 1991	95
Table 5-21.	Veterinary Expenditures, for Horses, per Year, 1987, 1991	96
Table 5-22.	Other Pet-Owning Households That Obtain Veterinary Care, 1991	97
Table 5-23.	Veterinary Visits and Expenditures for Other Pets, 1987, 1991	98

Chapter 6   **Veterinary Medical Profession**   **99**

Table 6-1.   Veterinarians, by State, 1980, 1990, 1991   101
Table 6-2.   Veterinarians, by Gender, 1980, 1990, 1991   105
Table 6-3.   Veterinarians, by Age, 1980, 1990, 1991   106
Table 6-4.   Veterinarians, by Primary Employment, 1980, 1990, 1991   109
Table 6-5.   Veterinarians, by Year of Graduation, 1980, 1990, 1991   114

Appendix A   **Study Methodology**   **117**

Table A-1.   Sample Representativeness: Household Characteristics   120
Table A-2.   Sample Representativeness: Geographic Division   121
Table A-3.   Sample Representativeness: Population Density   121
Table A-4.   Sample Representativeness: Age of Head of Household   122
Table A-5.   Sample Representativeness: Annual Household Income   123
Table A-6.   Sample Representativeness: Size of Household   123

List of Figures

Chapter 1	**Population of Pets**	1
Figure 1-1.	Pet Ownership Among US Households, 1991	1
Figure 1-2.	Percentage of Households, by Region, That Owned Pets, 1991	2
Figure 1-3.	Percentage of Households Owning a Pet, 1987, 1991	3
Figure 1-4.	Pet Population, 1987, 1991	4
Figure 1-5.	Percentage of Households, by State, That Owned Dogs, 1991	6
Figure 1-6.	Number of Dogs Owned by Households, 1991	9
Figure 1-7.	Percentage of Dogs Owned by Age of Dog, 1987, 1991	10
Figure 1-8.	Percentage of Households, by State, That Owned Cats, 1991	11
Figure 1-9.	Number of Cats Owned by Households, 1991	14
Figure 1-10.	Percentage of Cats Owned by Age of Cat, 1987, 1991	15
Figure 1-11.	Percentage of Households, by Region, That Owned Birds, 1991	17
Figure 1-12.	Number of Birds Owned by Households, 1991	18
Figure 1-13.	Percentage of Birds Owned by Age of Bird, 1987, 1991	19
Figure 1-14.	Percentage of Households, by Region, That Owned Horses, 1991	21
Figure 1-15.	Number of Horses Owned by Households, 1991	22
Figure 1-16.	Percentage of Horses Owned by Age of Horse, 1987, 1991	23
Chapter 2	**Breed of Pets**	27
Figure 2-1.	Registration Numbers of Top Five Dog Breeds, 1982, 1992	31
Figure 2-2.	Registration Numbers of Top Five Cat Breeds, 1982, 1992	34
Chapter 3	**Pet Demographics**	35
Figure 3-1.	Demographics of Pet Ownership, by Life-stage, 1991	36
Figure 3-2.	Demographics of Pet Ownership, by Household Size, 1991	38
Figure 3-3.	Demographics of Dog Ownership, by Life-stage, 1991	40
Figure 3-4.	Demographics of Dog Ownership, by Household Size, 1991	41
Figure 3-5.	Demographics of Cat Ownership, by Life-stage, 1991	44
Figure 3-6.	Demographics of Cat Ownership, by Household Size, 1991	45
Figure 3-7.	Demographics of Bird Ownership, by Life-stage, 1991	48
Figure 3-8.	Demographics of Bird Ownership, by Household Size, 1991	49

Figure 3-9.	Demographics of Horse Ownership, by Life-stage, 1991	52
Figure 3-10.	Demographics of Horse Ownership, by Household Size, 1991	53

Chapter 4 — Profiles of Pet-owning Households — 55

Figure 4-1.	Profile of Pet-Owning Households, by Life-stage, 1991	56
Figure 4-2.	Profile of Pet-Owning Households, by Household Size, 1991	58
Figure 4-3.	Profile of Dog-Owning Households, by Life-stage, 1991	63
Figure 4-4.	Profile of Dog-Owning Households, by Household Size, 1991	65
Figure 4-5.	Profile of Cat-Owning Households, by Life-stage, 1991	67
Figure 4-6.	Profile of Cat-Owning Households, by Household Size, 1991	68
Figure 4-7.	Profile of Bird-Owning Households, by Life-stage, 1991	71
Figure 4-8.	Profile of Bird-Owning Households, by Household Size, 1991	72
Figure 4-9.	Profile of Horse-Owning Households, by Life-stage, 1991	75
Figure 4-10.	Profile of Horse-Owning Households, by Household Size, 1991	77

Chapter 5 — Pet Food and Veterinary Services for Pets — 79

Figure 5-1.	Age and Gender of Person Responsible for Pet Care, 1991	80
Figure 5-2.	Veterinary Visits, for Dogs, per Year, 1983, 1987, 1991	85
Figure 5-3.	Veterinary Expenditures, for Dogs, per Year, 1983, 1987, 1991	86
Figure 5-4.	Veterinary Visits, for Cats, per Year, 1983, 1987, 1991	89
Figure 5-5.	Veterinary Expenditures, for Cats, per Year, 1983, 1987, 1991	90

Chapter 6 — Veterinary Medical Profession — 99

Figure 6-1.	Veterinarians, 1980, 1990, 1991	100
Figure 6-2.	Percentage Change in the Number of Veterinarians, by State, 1980 - 1990	100
Figure 6-3.	Veterinarians, by Division, 1980 & 1990	103
Figure 6-4.	Veterinarians, by Division, 1991	104
Figure 6-5.	Veterinarians, by Gender, 1980, 1990, 1991	105
Figure 6-6.	Veterinarians, by Age, 1980 & 1990	107
Figure 6-7.	Veterinarians, by Age, 1991	107
Figure 6-8.	Veterinarians, by Primary Employment, 1980 & 1990	110
Figure 6-9.	Veterinarians, by Primary Employment, 1991	111
Figure 6-10.	Veterinarians, by Veterinary Medical College, 1991	113
Figure 6-11.	Veterinarians, by Year of Graduation, 1991	115

CHAPTER 1

Population of Pets

■ PET OWNERSHIP

Approximately 54.8 million households, 57.9% of all US households, own a companion animal (Figure 1-1). Companion animals include dogs, cats, birds, horses, or any of several other pets, such as hamsters, gerbils, fish, and rabbits.

Figure 1-1. Pet Ownership Among US Households, 1991

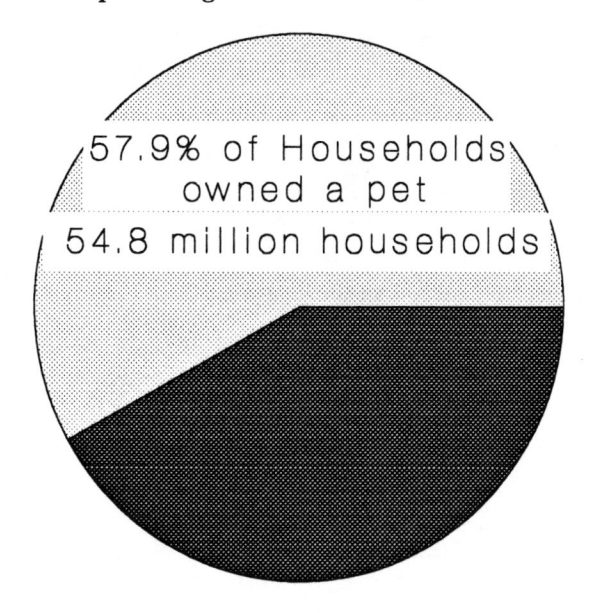

57.9% of Households owned a pet
54.8 million households

Companion animal ownership varies with geographic region of the country, ranging from a low of 51.8% in the Middle Atlantic region to a high of 64.8% in the West South Central region (Figure 1-2). Approximately 63% of households in the Mountain and Pacific regions own companion animals, compared to less than 60% of households in the New England, Middle Atlantic, South Atlantic, East North Central, West North Central, and East South Central regions.

Population of Pets

Figure 1-2. Percentage of Households, by Region, That Owned Pets, 1991

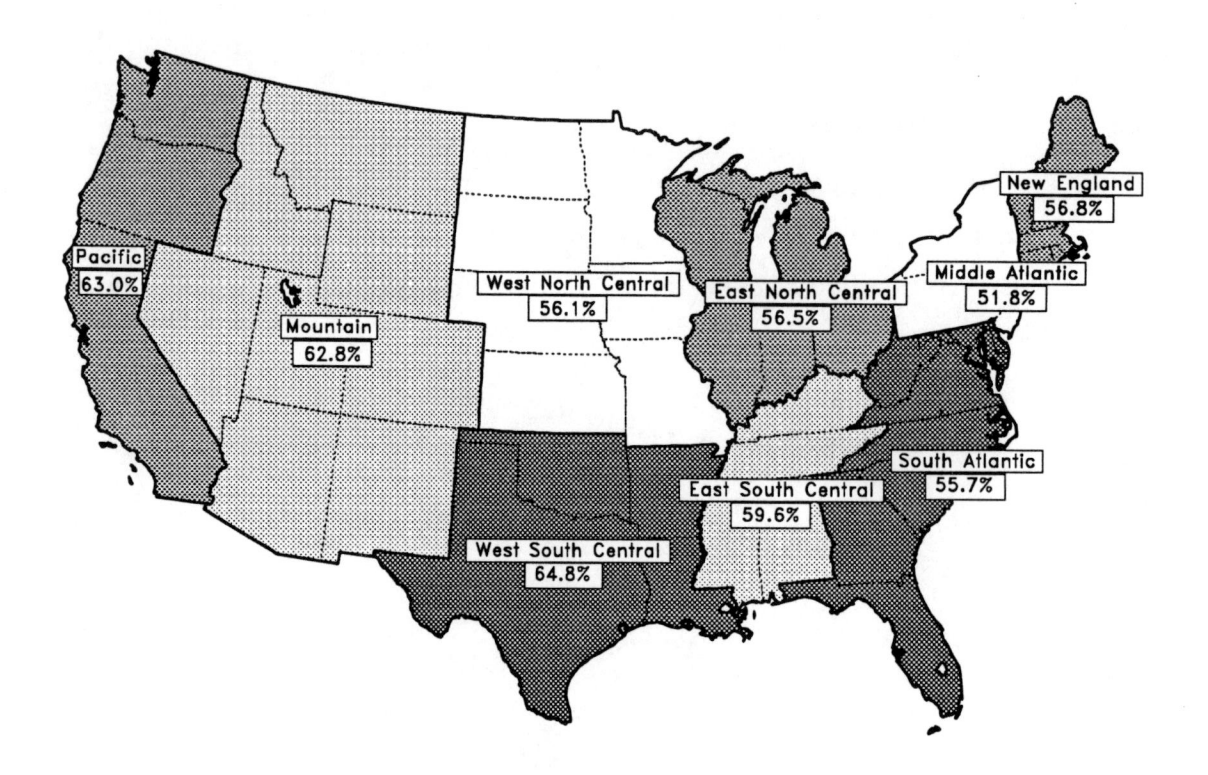

Region	Percentage
Pacific	63.0%
Mountain	62.8%
West North Central	56.1%
West South Central	64.8%
East North Central	56.5%
East South Central	59.6%
New England	56.8%
Middle Atlantic	51.8%
South Atlantic	55.7%

The overall number of dogs owned by Americans and the number of households owning dogs have not changed since 1987. Approximately 34.6 million households own a dog (Table 1-1). Whereas, 34.7 million households owned a dog in 1987 (references at end of chapter). Because the total number of US households grew during this time, the percentage of households that own dogs decreased from 38.2% in 1987 to 36.5% in 1991 (Figure 1-3). On the basis of 1.52 dogs owned per dog-owning household, the dog population for 1991 is estimated to be 52.5 million dogs, and for 1987 is estimated to be 52.4 million dogs.

Table 1-1. Pet Ownership and Population Estimates, 1987, 1991

	Households That Own a Pet (Percent) 1987	1991	Number of Households (Millions) 1987	1991	Mean Number Owned per Household 1987	1991	Pet Population (Millions) 1987	1991
Dogs	38.2	36.5	34.7	34.6	1.51	1.52	52.4	52.5
Cats	30.5	30.9	27.7	29.2	2.04	1.95	54.6	57.0
Birds	5.7	5.7	5.2	5.4	2.48	2.16	12.9	11.7
Horses	2.8	2.0	2.6	1.9	2.63	2.54	6.6	4.9
Other pets	—	6.7	—	6.3	—	—	—	—

Figure 1-3. Percentage of Households Owning a Pet, 1987, 1991

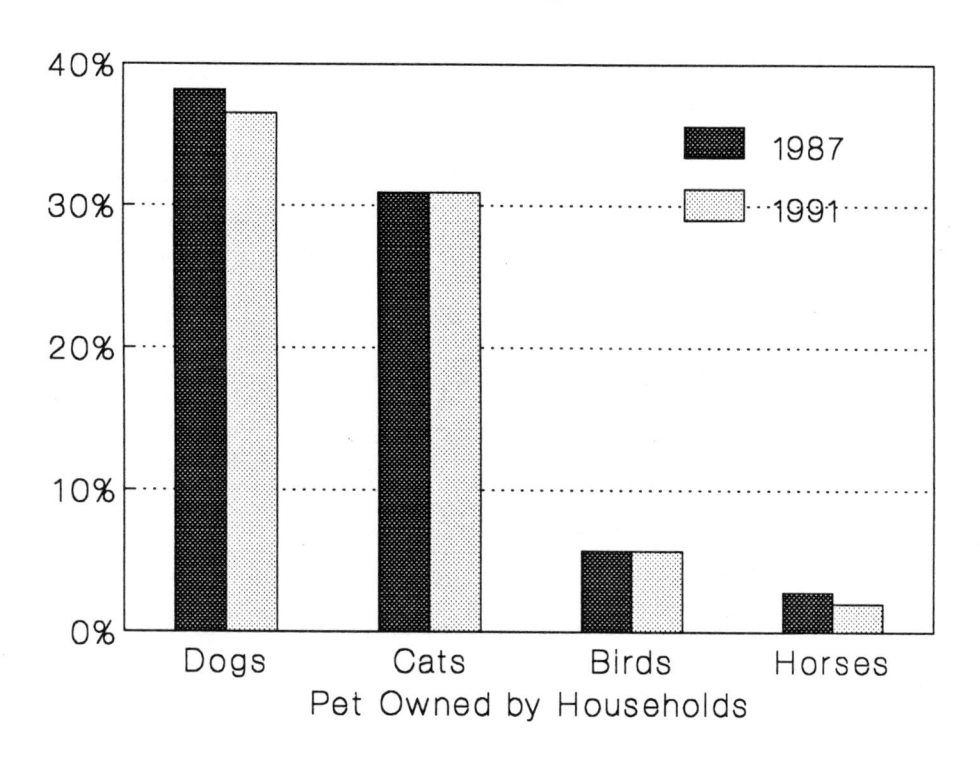

Population of Pets

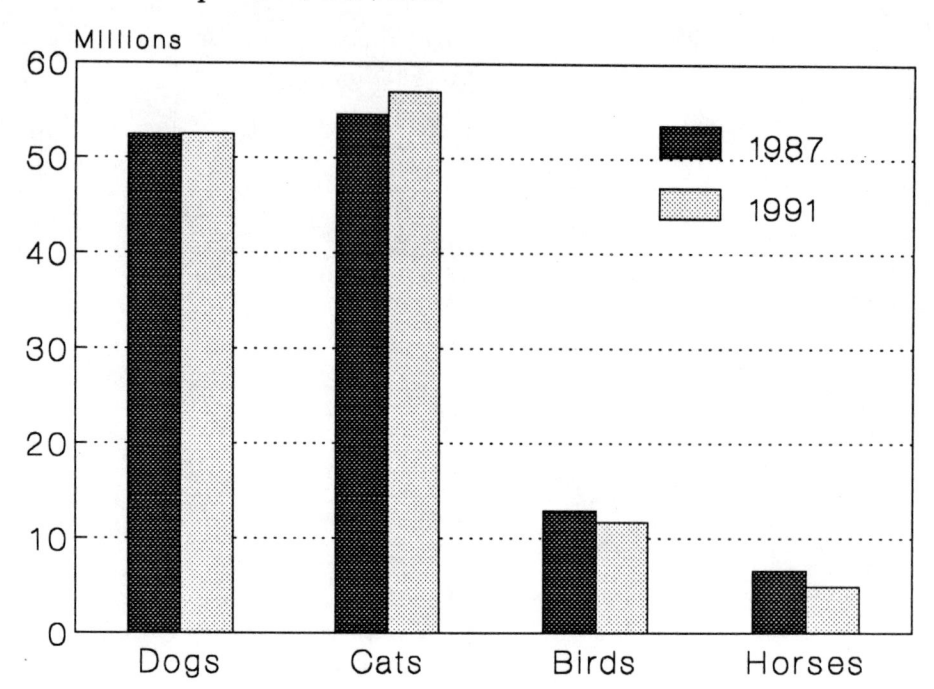

Figure 1-4. Pet Population, 1987, 1991

The cat population continues to grow. Approximately 29.2 million (30.9%) households own a cat, up slightly from 27.7 million (30.5%) households in 1987 (Table 1-1, Figure 1-3). On the basis of 1.95 cats owned per cat-owning household, the cat population for 1991 is estimated to be 57.0 million cats, an increase from 54.6 million cats in 1987 (Figure 1-4).

Pet bird population has decreased since 1987. About 5.4 million (5.7%) households own a bird, nearly unchanged from 5.2 million (5.7%) in 1987 (Table 1-1, Figure 1-3). On the basis of 2.16 birds owned per bird-owning household, the population of birds owned by households during 1991 is estimated to be 11.7 million birds, down from 12.9 million birds in 1987. This change may be due, in part, to a decrease in the mean number of birds owned per household (Table 1-1).

The estimated number of households that own a horse is 1.9 million (2.0%), a decrease from 2.6 million (2.8%) in 1987 (Table 1-1, Figure 1-3). The population of horses owned by households during 1991 is estimated to be 4.9 million horses, down from 6.6 million horses in 1987 (Figure 1-4). The mean number of horses owned per household is 2.54, a decrease from 2.63 in 1987.

Approximately 6.7% of US households own other pets, including an estimated 24.0 million fish, 4.6 million rabbits, 1.3 million hamsters, 600,000 gerbils, and several million other household pets of various species.

Many households own more than one type of pet. Table 1-2 shows the percentage of each type of pet-owning household that own, in addition, another type of pet.

Table 1-2. Percentage of Pet Owners That Owned Another Pet, 1991

Primary Pet	Dog	Cat	Bird	Horse
Dog	—	40.3	9.5	4.6
Cat	47.6	—	8.1	4.5
Bird	60.8	43.6	—	5.0
Horse	83.0	68.7	13.9	—

For instance, 40.3% of dog-owning households also own a cat and 47.6% of cat-owning households also own a dog. Eighty-three percent of horse-owning households also own a dog and nearly 69% also own a cat.

Population of Pets

■ DOG OWNERSHIP

For each state, the number of households that own a dog can be estimated by multiplying the percentage of households in that state that own a dog by the total number of households. The dog population can then be estimated by multiplying number of households by 1.52, the mean number of dogs owned per household.

Figure 1-5 illustrates the variation by state, in the percentage of households that own dogs. More than 44% of households in each of the following states own dogs: Arkansas, Nevada, New Mexico, Oklahoma, Texas, West Virginia, and Wyoming.

Figure 1-5. Percentage of Households, by State, That Owned Dogs, 1991

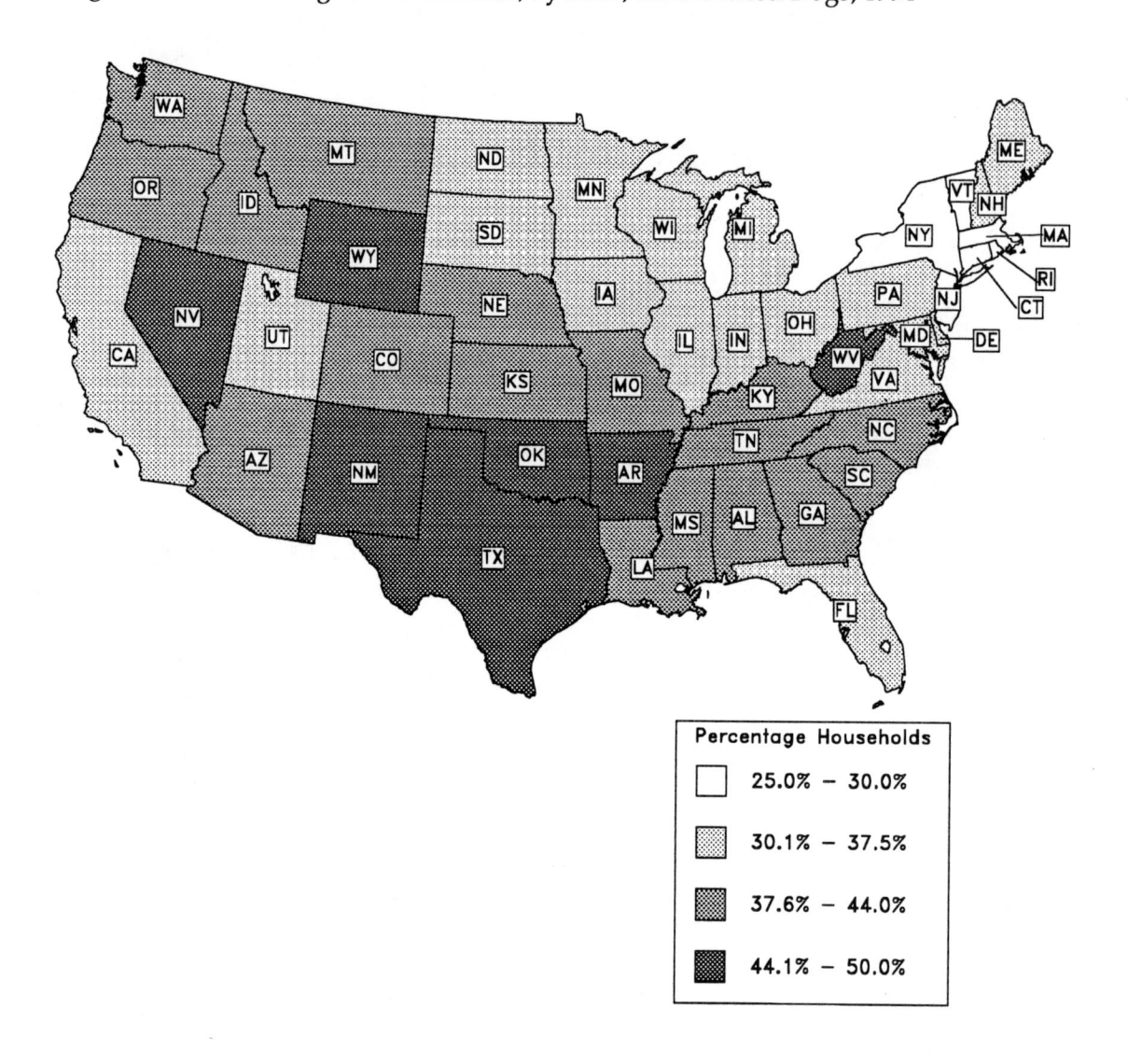

Table 1-3. Dog Ownership, by State, 1991

State	Households That Own a Dog (Percent)	Households That Own a Dog (Thousands)	Dog Population (Thousands)
US Total	36.5	34,565	52,539
New England	27.5	1,377	2,094
Maine	32.0	151	229
New Hampshire	33.5	139	212
Vermont	28.5	61	93
Massachusetts	25.2	575	873
Rhode Island	25.9	99	151
Connecticut	28.0	350	532
Middle Atlantic	29.3	4,142	6,297
New York	26.9	1,809	2,749
New Jersey	28.0	793	1,205
Pennsylvania	33.1	1,511	2,296
East North Central	35.6	5,640	8,574
Ohio	36.4	1,509	2,294
Indiana	37.0	775	1,178
Illinois	34.8	1,482	2,253
Michigan	37.2	1,291	1,962
Wisconsin	31.6	584	887
West North Central	37.0	2,525	3,838
Minnesota	32.6	545	829
Iowa	35.3	381	579
Missouri	40.4	803	1,221
North Dakota	33.1	81	123
South Dakota	30.6	80	122
Nebraska	41.8	255	388
Kansas	40.8	391	595
South Atlantic	35.6	5,960	9,059
Delaware	36.0	90	137
Maryland	31.9	567	861
Virginia	34.6	804	1,222
District of Columbia	13.2	33	51
West Virginia	48.0	336	510
North Carolina	39.4	1,006	1,529
South Carolina	41.2	526	799
Georgia	40.5	973	1,479
Florida	30.8	1,602	2,435

Population of Pets

Table 1-3. Dog Ownership, by State, 1991 (continued)

State	Households That Own a Dog (Percent)	(Thousands)	Dog Population (Thousands)
East South Central	42.7	2,447	3,719
Kentucky	42.0	588	894
Tennessee	43.5	818	1,243
Alabama	42.6	652	991
Mississippi	42.3	391	594
West South Central	47.5	4,662	7,086
Arkansas	48.2	435	662
Louisiana	40.4	614	934
Oklahoma	49.3	603	916
Texas	48.9	3,014	4,581
Mountain	42.7	2,178	3,311
Montana	43.9	136	207
Idaho	43.6	160	243
Wyoming	47.1	81	123
Colorado	43.5	565	859
New Mexico	47.2	260	396
Arizona	40.5	562	855
Utah	36.3	198	300
Nevada	46.6	220	335
Pacific	37.0	5,231	7,950
Washington	40.6	772	1,173
Oregon	42.3	474	720
California	35.7	3,756	5,708

The percentage of households that own a dog ranges from a low of 25.2% in Massachusetts to a high of 49.3% in Oklahoma (Table 1-3). In general, the New England region has the lowest percentage (27.5%) and the West South Central region has the highest percentage (47.5%) of dog-owning households. California has the largest population of dogs with 5.7 million dogs, followed by Texas with nearly 4.6 million dogs.

The majority (90%) of dog-owning households own one dog (Table 1-4); 30% own two or more dogs (Figure 1-6). The mean number of dogs owned per household is 1.52 dogs.

Table 1-4. Number of Dogs Owned by Households, 1983, 1987, 1991

Number of Dogs Owned	Percentage of Households		
	1983	1987	1991
One	70.0	69.7	70.2
Two	20.3	20.9	20.2
Three	5.3	5.9	5.6
Four or more	4.3	3.5	4.0

Figure 1-6. Number of Dogs Owned by Households, 1991

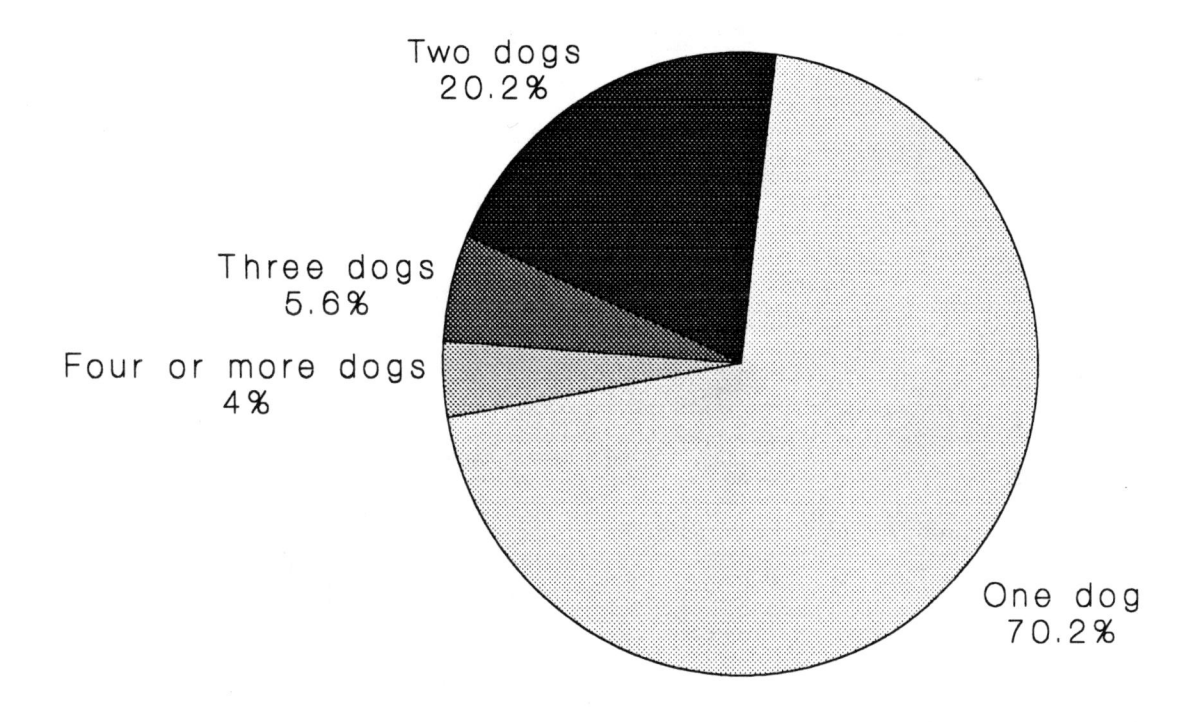

- Two dogs 20.2%
- Three dogs 5.6%
- Four or more dogs 4%
- One dog 70.2%

Population of Pets

Table 1-5. Percentage of Dogs Owned by Age of Dog, 1983, 1987, 1991

Age of Dog Owned	1983 (Pct.)	1987 (Pct.)	1991 (Pct.)
1 year or less	19.0	19.7	18.4
2 - 5 years	37.0	38.6	39.9
6 - 10 years	27.0	27.1	27.8
11 years or greater	12.0	14.6	13.9
Don't know	5.0	—	—

The largest percentage (40%) of the dogs owned are between 2 to 5 years old (Table 1-5). The next largest age group of dogs (28%) is the 6 to 10 year old age group. Approximately 18% of dogs are less than one year old and 14% are more than eleven years old (Figure 1-7).

Figure 1-7. Percentage of Dogs Owned by Age of Dog, 1987, 1991

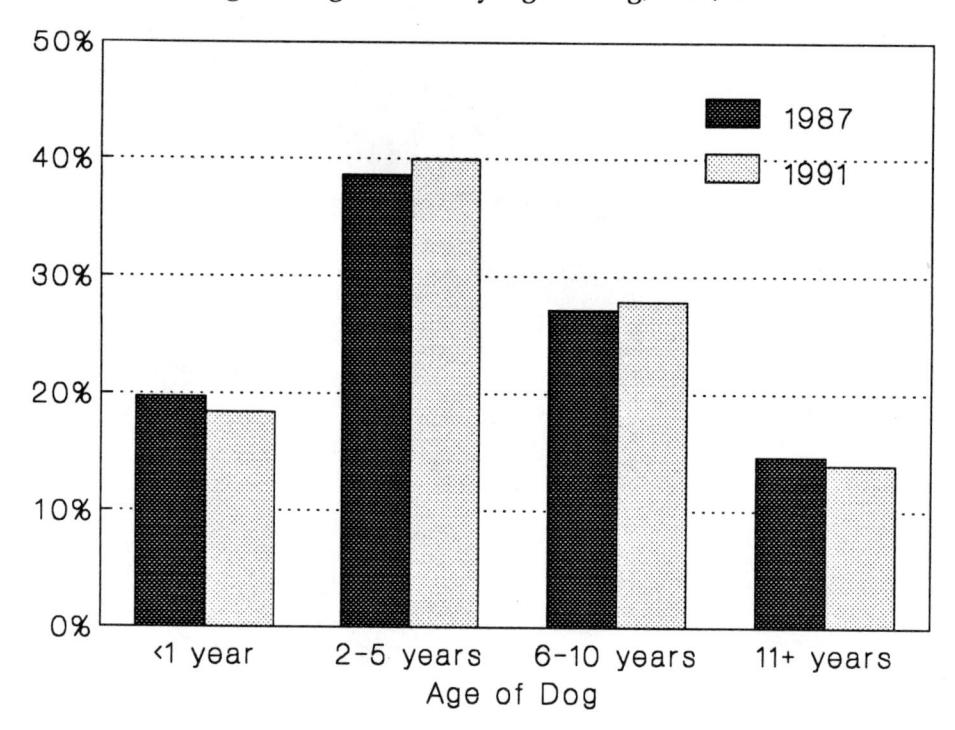

■ CAT OWNERSHIP

For each state, the number of households that own a cat can be estimated by multiplying the percentage of households in that state that own a cat by the total number of households. The cat population can then be estimated by multiplying number of households by 1.95, the mean number of cats owned per household.

Figure 1-8 illustrates the variation, by state, in the percentage of households that own cats. More than 37% of households in Idaho, Maine, Montana, Oregon, Vermont, and Washington own cats.

Figure 1-8. Percentage of Households, by State, That Owned Cats, 1991

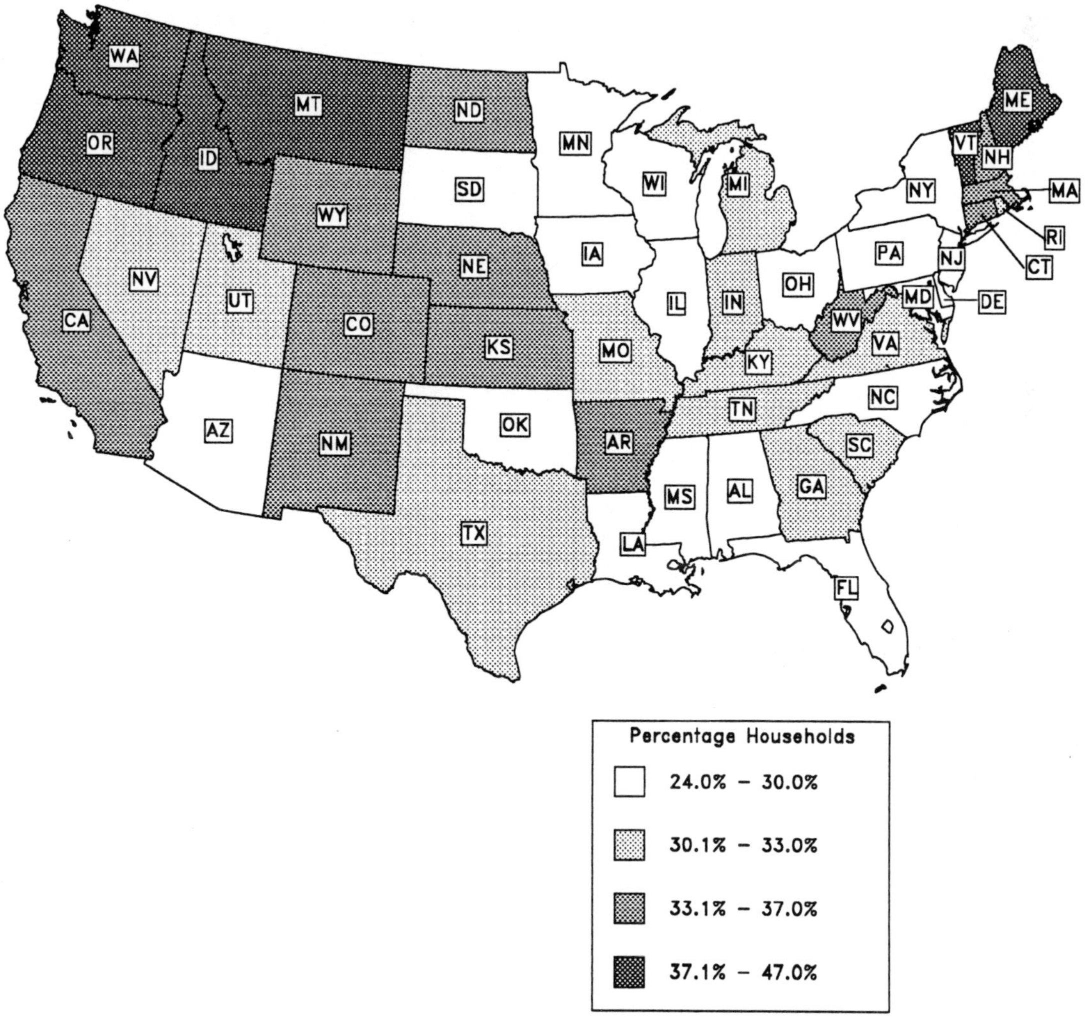

Percentage Households
- 24.0% – 30.0%
- 30.1% – 33.0%
- 33.1% – 37.0%
- 37.1% – 47.0%

Population of Pets

Table 1-6. Cat Ownership, by State, 1991

State	Households That Own a Cat (Percent)	(Thousands)	Cat Population (Thousands)
US Total	30.9	29,219	56,977
New England	35.8	1,796	3,503
Maine	44.0	208	405
New Hampshire	36.3	151	295
Vermont	46.9	100	196
Massachusetts	34.4	785	1,531
Rhode Island	30.4	116	227
Connecticut	35.1	439	855
Middle Atlantic	27.0	3,820	7,449
New York	27.6	1,858	3,622
New Jersey	25.5	724	1,412
Pennsylvania	27.2	1,239	2,416
East North Central	28.5	4,503	8,781
Ohio	29.4	1,218	2,374
Indiana	31.4	658	1,284
Illinois	26.5	1,129	2,202
Michigan	30.1	1,042	2,033
Wisconsin	24.5	452	881
West North Central	31.0	2,116	4,126
Minnesota	28.8	481	937
Iowa	29.8	321	626
Missouri	30.6	608	1,186
North Dakota	35.0	85	167
South Dakota	27.6	73	142
Nebraska	35.5	217	422
Kansas	34.6	332	647
South Atlantic	28.4	4,760	9,281
Delaware	29.7	74	145
Maryland	28.2	501	977
Virginia	32.3	751	1,465
District of Columbia	21.7	55	107
West Virginia	34.7	242	472
North Carolina	26.3	671	1,307
South Carolina	31.7	405	789
Georgia	31.3	751	1,464
Florida	25.1	1,308	2,550

Table 1-6. Cat Ownership, by State, 1991 (continued)

State	Households That Own a Cat (Percent)	(Thousands)	Cat Population (Thousands)
East South Central	30.1	1,724	3,362
Kentucky	30.3	425	828
Tennessee	32.4	609	1,187
Alabama	27.1	414	807
Mississippi	29.8	275	537
West South Central	32.0	3,139	6,120
Arkansas	36.5	330	643
Louisiana	28.6	435	848
Oklahoma	29.2	358	697
Texas	32.7	2,015	3,930
Mountain	33.2	1,694	3,302
Montana	40.2	125	244
Idaho	43.1	158	308
Wyoming	34.6	59	116
Colorado	35.6	463	903
New Mexico	34.6	191	372
Arizona	26.5	368	717
Utah	32.9	179	350
Nevada	32.5	154	300
Pacific	37.5	5,285	10,305
Washington	43.5	826	1,610
Oregon	46.2	517	1,009
California	35.1	3,694	7,203

The Pacific region has the largest cat population with 37.5% of households owning cats, somewhat higher than the national average of 30.9%. In the Middle Atlantic region, 27% of households own cats (Table 1-6). The percentage of cat-owning households in each state ranges from 46.9% in Vermont to 24.5% in Wisconsin.

Population of Pets

The majority of households (58%) own one cat (Table 1-7); 32% own two or three cats, and 10% own four or more cats (Figure 1-9). The mean number of cats owned per household is 1.95 cats.

Table 1-7. Number of Cats Owned by Households, 1983, 1987, 1991

Number of Cats Owned	Percentage of Households		
	1983	1987	1991
One	59.1	57.4	57.8
Two	20.4	24.4	23.9
Three	8.2	8.2	8.1
Four or more	12.4	10.0	10.2

Figure 1-9. Number of Cats Owned by Households, 1991

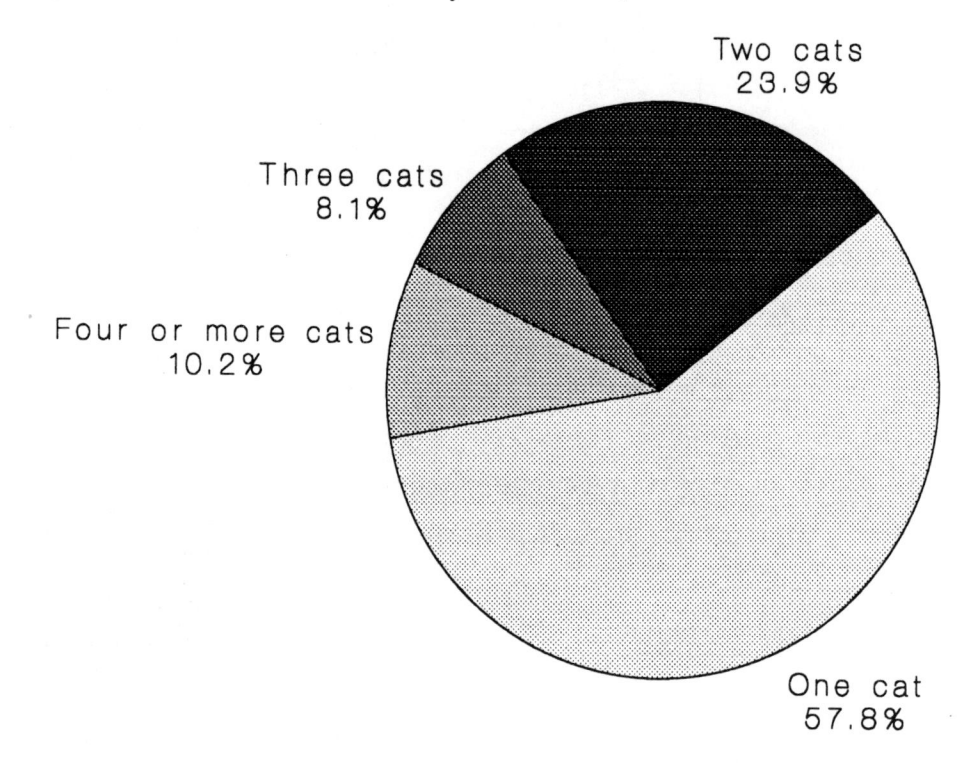

AVMA Center for Information Management

Table 1-8. Percentage of Cats Owned by Age of Cat, 1983, 1987, 1991

Age of Cat Owned	1983 (Pct.)	1987 (Pct.)	1991 (Pct.)
1 year or less	27.0	28.1	22.5
2 - 5 years	38.0	43.4	44.1
6 - 10 years	16.0	17.9	22.4
11 years or greater	8.0	10.6	11.0
Don't know	11.0	—	—

Households are owning older cats (Table 1-8). Thirty-three percent of cats that are owned are over six years old, compared with 28% in 1987. Twenty-two percent of cats that are owned are less than one year old, compared with 28% of households in 1987 (Figure 1-10).

Figure 1-10. Percentage of Cats Owned by Age of Cat, 1987, 1991

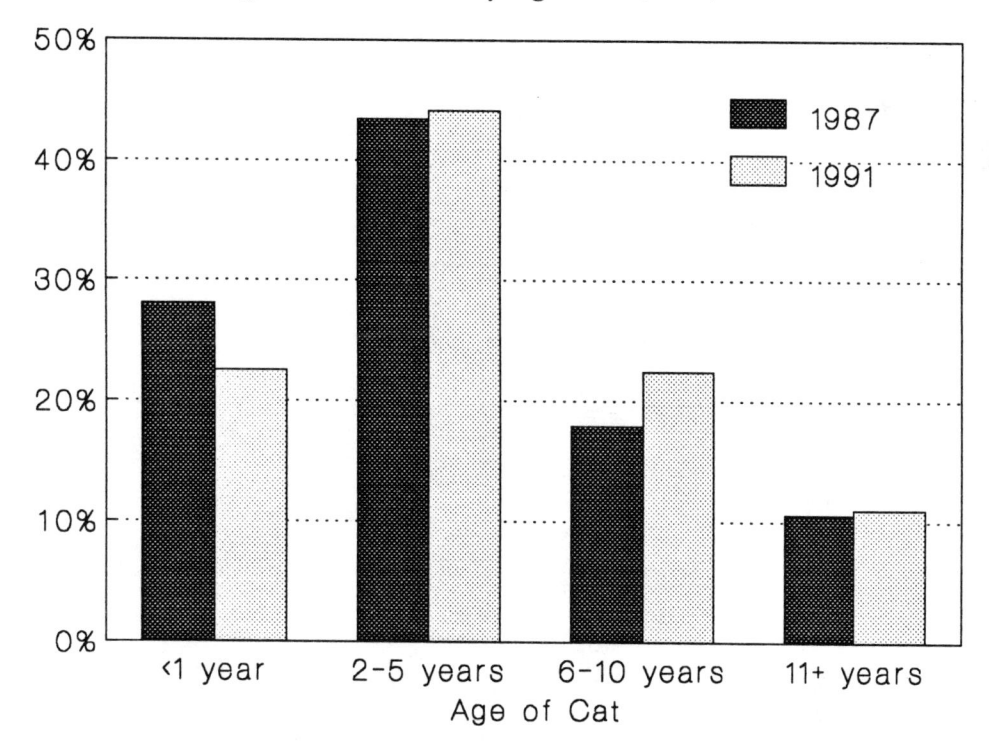

Population of Pets

■ BIRD OWNERSHIP

Pet bird ownership was analyzed by region, rather than by state, because available research data on birds were insufficiently valid to develop estimated populations at the state level. The pet-bird population is highest in the Pacific region, where 8.3% of the households own birds (Table 1-9). In the West North Central region, 4.1% of the households own birds, the lowest percentage among all regions (Figure 1-11).

Table 1-9. Bird Ownership, by Region, 1991

Region	Households That Own a Bird (Percent)	(Thousands)	Bird Population (Thousands)
US Total	5.7	5,413	11,692
New England	4.4	219	472
Middle Atlantic	5.4	766	1,655
East North Central	5.2	830	1,792
West North Central	4.1	277	598
South Atlantic	5.7	952	2,056
East South Central	4.4	250	540
West South Central	6.0	584	1,262
Mountain	6.1	313	676
Pacific	8.3	1,167	2,522

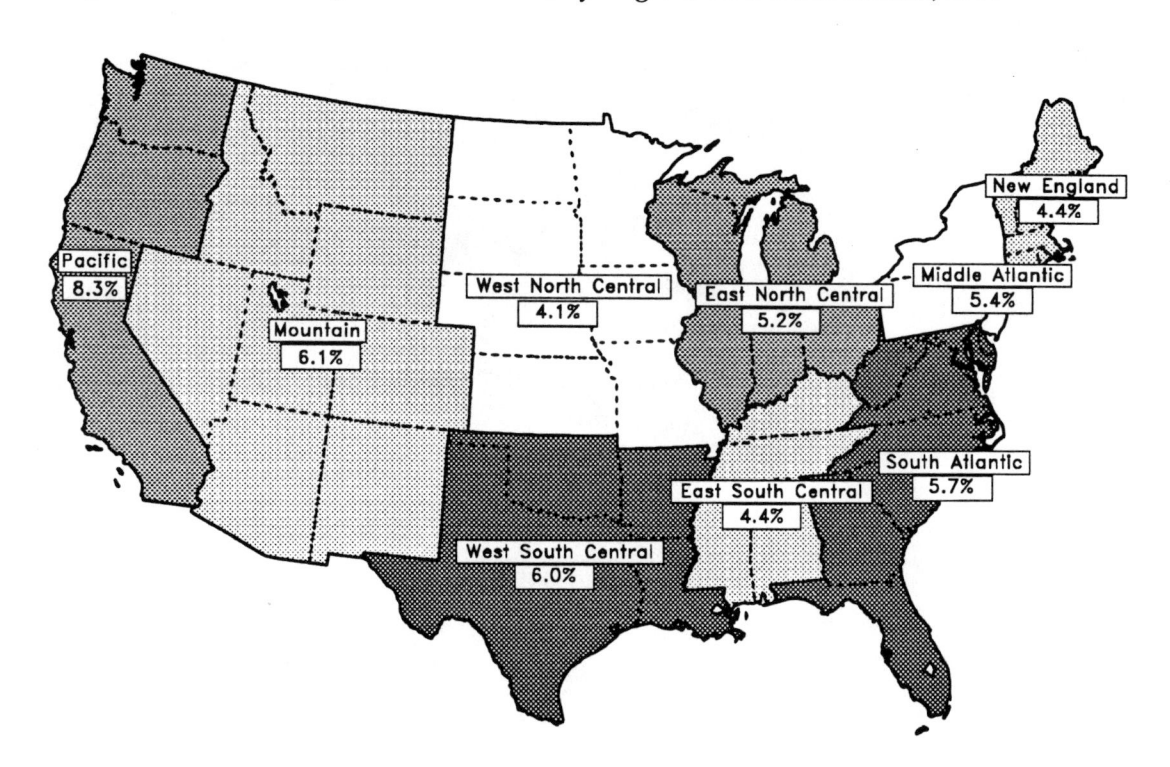

Figure 1-11. Percentage of Households, by Region, That Owned Birds, 1991

- New England 4.4%
- Middle Atlantic 5.4%
- Pacific 8.3%
- West North Central 4.1%
- East North Central 5.2%
- Mountain 6.1%
- South Atlantic 5.7%
- East South Central 4.4%
- West South Central 6.0%

The majority (65.1%) of bird-owning households own one bird (Table 1-10); 35% own two or more birds (Figure 1-12). The mean number of birds owned per household is 2.16 birds.

Table 1-10. Number of Birds Owned by Households, 1987, 1991

Number of Birds Owned	Percentage of Households 1987	Percentage of Households 1991
One	63.5	65.6
Two	21.7	20.7
Three	4.8	4.7
Four or more	10.0	9.0

Population of Pets

Figure 1-12. Number of Birds Owned by Households, 1991

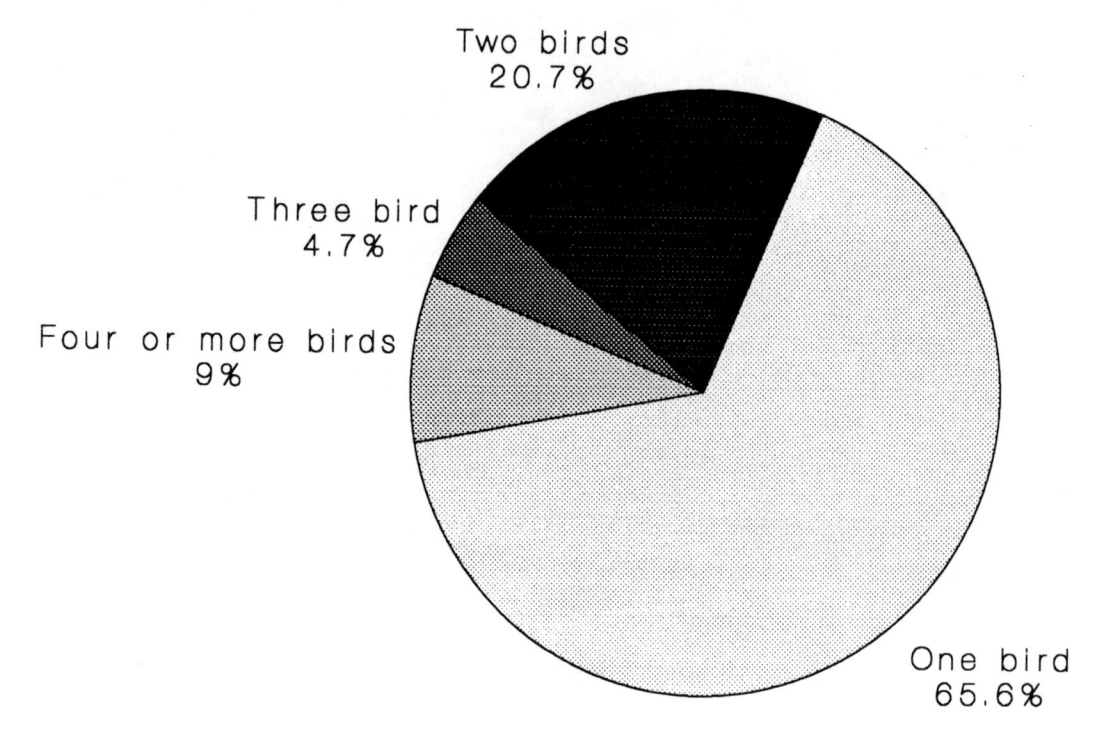

- Two birds 20.7%
- Three bird 4.7%
- Four or more birds 9%
- One bird 65.6%

Eighty percent of pet birds are less than five years old. Half of the birds owned by households are between 2 and 5 years old (Table 1-11). Thirty percent of pet birds owned are less than one year old and 19% are more than six years old (Figure 1-13).

Table 1-11. Percentage of Birds Owned by Age of Bird, 1987, 1991

Age of Bird Owned	1987 (Pct.)	1991 (Pct.)
1 year or less	32.9	30.4
2 - 5 years	51.8	50.8
6 - 10 years	9.6	13.7
11 years or greater	5.7	5.1

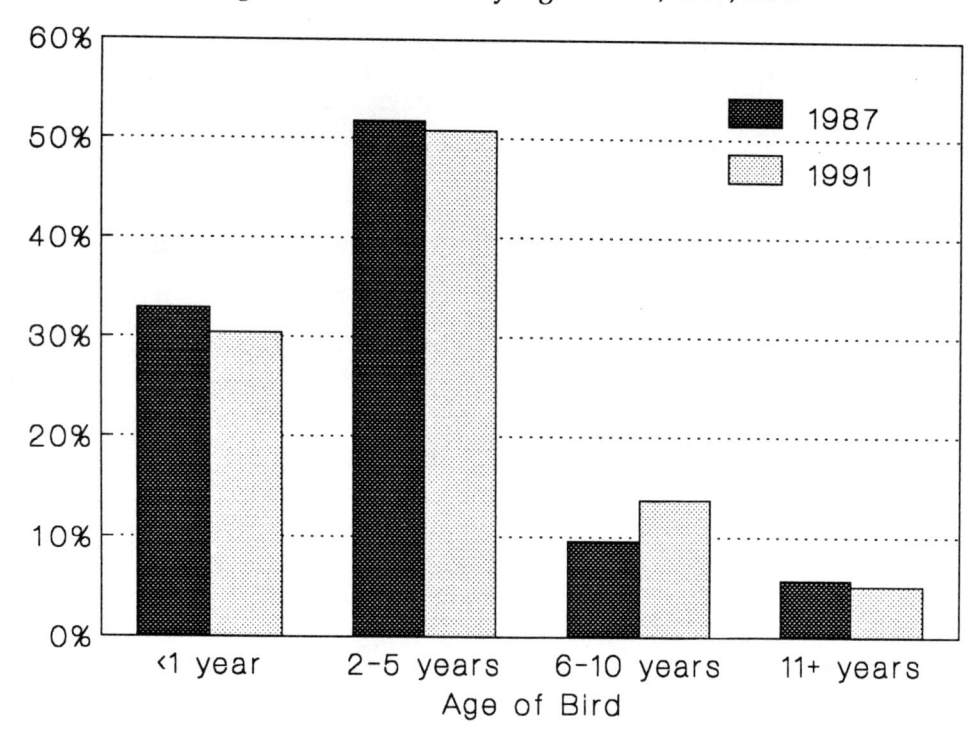

Figure 1-13. Percentage of Birds Owned by Age of Bird, 1987, 1991

Population of Pets

■ HORSE OWNERSHIP

Horse population estimates, presented on a regional basis, reveal small percentages of households owning horses. The percentage of horse-owning households range from 4.4% of households in the Mountain region to 0.8% of households in the Middle Atlantic region. The West South Central region has the largest population of horses with 827,000. The New England region has a population of only 139,000 horses, the smallest among the regions (Table 1-12).

Horses owned by commercial or other non-household establishments are not included in the population estimate.

Table 1-12. Horse Ownership, by Region, 1991

Region	Households That Own a Horse (Percent)	(Thousands)	Horse Population (Thousands)
US Total	2.0	1,925	4,890
New England	1.1	55	139
Middle Atlantic	0.8	116	295
East North Central	1.4	228	580
West North Central	2.8	190	483
South Atlantic	1.8	307	781
East South Central	2.6	146	371
West South Central	3.3	326	827
Mountain	4.4	222	564
Pacific	2.3	321	815

Figure 1-14 on the following page illustrates the horse population by region.

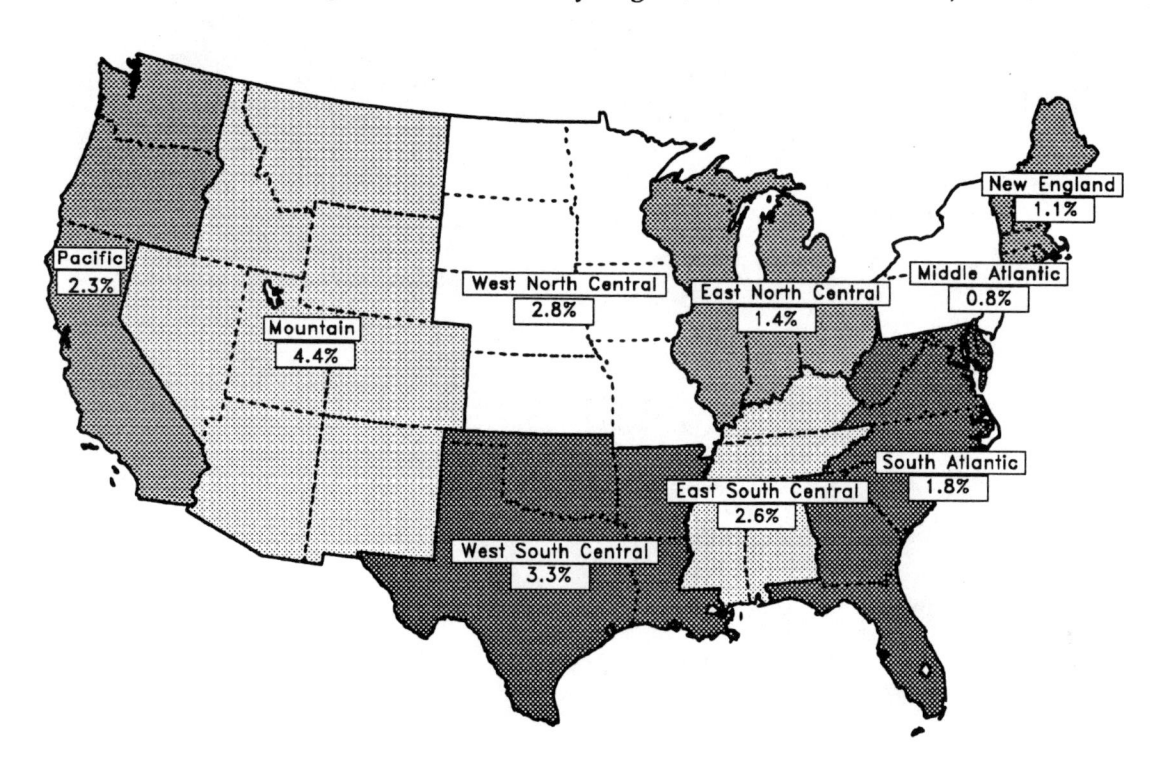

Figure 1-14. Percentage of Households, by Region, That Owned Horses, 1991

- Pacific: 2.3%
- Mountain: 4.4%
- West North Central: 2.8%
- East North Central: 1.4%
- New England: 1.1%
- Middle Atlantic: 0.8%
- West South Central: 3.3%
- East South Central: 2.6%
- South Atlantic: 1.8%

Nearly half of the horse-owning households own one horse. Specifically, 48.3% of households own one horse, compared with 44.3% in 1987 (Table 1-13). Seventeen percent of households own four or more horses in 1991 and in 1987 (Figure 1-15).

Table 1-13. Number of Horses Owned by Households, 1987, 1991

Number of Horses Owned	Percent of Households 1987	Percent of Households 1991
One	44.3	48.3
Two	27.2	23.3
Three	10.7	11.2
Four or more	17.8	17.3

Population of Pets

Figure 1-15. Number of Horses Owned by Households, 1991

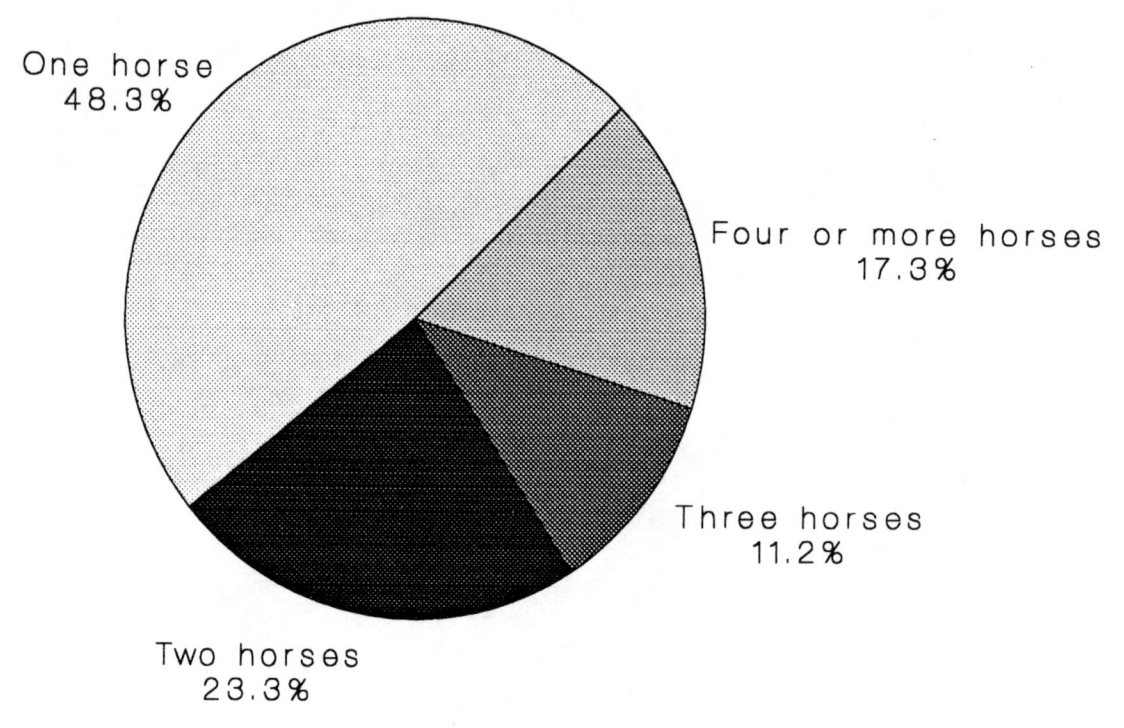

- One horse 48.3%
- Four or more horses 17.3%
- Three horses 11.2%
- Two horses 23.3%

Households are owning older horses and this decrease is associated with a downward trend in horse population. The percentage of horses owned by households less than one year of age is 8.6%, a decline from 1987 when 12.6% of horses were less than one year old (Table 1-14). The percentage of horses over six years old increased from 54.5% in 1987 to 64.9% in 1991. Figure 1-16 graphically illustrates the change in age distribution.

Table 1-14. Percentage of Horses Owned by Age of Horse, 1983, 1987, 1991

Age of Horse Owned	1983 (Pct.)	1987 (Pct.)	1991 (Pct.)
1 year or less	10.0	12.6	8.6
2 - 5 years	31.0	32.9	26.5
6 - 10 years	29.0	27.0	30.2
11 years or greater	30.0	27.5	34.7

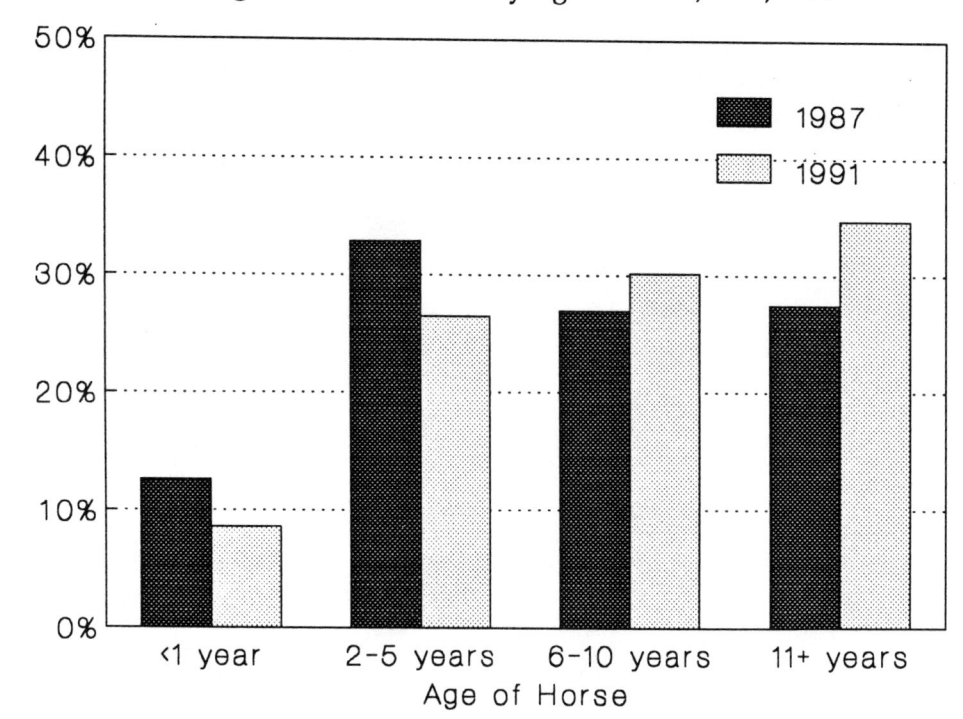

Figure 1-16. Percentage of Horses Owned by Age of Horse, 1987, 1991

Population of Pets

■ OTHER PETS OWNERSHIP

A number of other companion animals are owned by US households. Approximately 8.7% of US households own other pets, a slight decrease from 8.9% in 1987. Specifically, 2.8% of households own fish; 1.5%, rabbits; 1.8%, rodents (hamsters, guinea pigs, and gerbils); 0.2%, ferrets; 0.9%, all reptiles; and 0.9%, other birds (eg, ducks, geese) and livestock (Table 1-15).

Table 1-15. Percentage of Households That Owned Other Pets, 1983, 1987, 1991

Other Pets	1983 (Pct.)	1987 (Pct.)	1991 (Pct.)
Fish	7.3	2.8	2.8
Rabbit	1.7	1.7	1.5
Hamster	0.7	1.1	1.0
Guinea Pig	0.5	0.5	0.5
Gerbil	0.5	0.4	0.3
Ferret	—	0.2	0.2
Other Rodents	0.2	0.4	0.4
Turtle	—	0.4	0.4
Snake	—	0.1	0.2
Lizard	—	0.1	0.2
Other Reptiles	0.5	0.1	0.1
Other Birds	0.4	0.5	0.4
Livestock	—	0.4	0.5
All Others	—	0.2	0.2

Fish owners have, on average, nine fish per household. Given that there are about 2.6 million fish-owning households, the pet fish population is approximately 24 million (Table 1-16).

Estimated populations for other pet species include:
4.5 million rabbits; 2.8 million hamsters, guinea pigs, and gerbils; and 275,000 ferrets.

Table 1-16. Other Pet Ownership, 1991

Other Pets	Other Pets/ Household (No.)	Households Owning Pets (Thousands)	Pet Population (Thousands)
Fish	9.05	2,652	23,997
Rabbit	3.22	1,420	4,574
Hamster	1.39	947	1,316
Guinea Pig	1.77	473	838
Gerbil	2.18	284	619
Ferret	1.45	189	275
Other Rodents	2.31	379	875
Turtle	1.87	379	708
Snake	3.88	189	735
Lizard	1.66	189	314
Other Reptiles	2.97	95	281
Other Birds	13.78	379	5,220
Livestock	7.12	473	3,371
All Others	3.37	189	638

References:

1) The Veterinary Service Market for Companion Animals, 1992. American Veterinary Medical Association, October, 1992.

2) The Veterinary Service Market for Companion Animals, 1988. American Veterinary Medical Association, August, 1988.

3) The Veterinary Service Market Study, 1983. American Veterinary Medical Association, July, 1983.

CHAPTER 2

Breeds of Pets

■ DOG BREEDS

The American Kennel Club, Inc. compiles registration numbers for 135 dog breeds. In 1992, The American Kennel Club processed about 1.4 million new dog registrations.

During the years 1992 and 1982, Labrador Retrievers, Cocker Spaniels, German Shepherd Dogs, and Poodles were among the top five dog breeds in terms of numbers of new dogs registered. In the past decade, Doberman Pinschers dropped from being the third most popular breed in terms of new registrations to being the twentieth most popular. There was a tremendous increase in the number of Rottweilers registered, and Rottweillers replaced Doberman Pinschers in the list of the top five breeds.

Labrador Retrievers had the largest number of new registrations in 1992 with 120,879 dogs registered. In 1982, there were 62,465 Labrador Retrievers registered, ranking fourth highest in registration numbers. Rottweilers jumped in numbers from 9,269 dogs registered (27th place) in 1982 to 95,445 dogs registered (2nd place) in 1992. Cocker Spaniels, the second most popular breed in 1982 with 87,218 dogs registered, dropped to third place in 1992 even though the number of Cocker Spaniels registered increased to 91,925. There were 76,941 German Shepherd Dogs registered in 1992, making them the fourth most popular breed, an increase from fifth place in 1982 when 60,445 dogs were registered. Poodles were the most popular dog breed in 1982 with 88,650 dogs registered, but only the fifth most popular breed in 1992 with 73,449 dogs registered.

Table 2-1 lists the breeds in rank order by number of dogs registered during 1992.

Pet Breeds

Table 2-1. Dogs Registered by The American Kennel Club Inc., 1982, 1992

Breed	1992 Rank	1992 No.	1982 Rank	1982 No.
Labrador Retrievers	1	120,879	4	62,465
Rottweilers	2	95,445	27	9,269
Cocker Spaniels	3	91,925	2	87,218
German Shepherd Dogs	4	76,941	5	60,445
Poodles	5	73,449	1	88,650
Golden Retrievers	6	69,850	6	51,045
Beagles	7	60,661	8	35,548
Dachshunds	8	50,046	9	32,835
Shetland Sheepdogs	9	43,449	10	30,512
Chow Chows	10	42,670	13	22,623
Shih Tzu	11	42,561	16	20,556
Pomeranians	12	42,488	18	18,456
Miniature Schnauzers	13	41,058	7	36,502
Yorkshire Terriers	14	39,904	11	26,205
Dalmatians	15	38,927	40	5,409
Chihuahuas	16	31,301	23	15,867
Boxers	17	30,123	22	16,301
Siberian Huskies	18	26,057	15	20,654
English Springer Spaniels	19	22,183	14	22,296
Doberman Pinschers	20	22,113	3	73,180
Basset Hounds	21	21,137	19	17,871
Lhasa Apsos	22	20,616	12	25,945
Pekingese	23	18,218	20	17,434
Maltese	24	17,615	30	8,050
Boston Terriers	25	17,271	25	11,361
Collies	26	17,081	17	20,084
Pugs	27	16,008	37	6,058
Brittanys	28	14,901	21	17,349
German Shorthaired Pointers	29	13,737	26	10,019
Miniature Pinschers	30	13,353	52	2,193
Bichons Frises	31	12,172	48	3,632
Bulldogs	32	12,046	35	6,657
Akitas	33	11,383	46	3,257
Great Danes	34	11,067	24	12,092
West Highland White Terriers	35	10,015	32	7,397
Scottish Terriers	36	7,914	39	5,834
Samoyeds	37	7,267	31	7,862
Pembroke Welsh Corgis	38	6,501	50	2,575
Keeshonden	39	6,177	38	5,977
Cairn Terriers	40	6,141	36	6,108
Alaskan Malamutes	41	5,644	33	7,209
Chesapeake Bay Retrievers	42	5,295	44	4,243
Saint Bernards	43	4,863	45	4,296
Weimaraners	44	4,758	41	4,586
Airedale Terriers	45	4,236	34	6,876
Great Pyrenees	46	3,776	54	1,684
Schipperkes	47	3,752	56	1,569
Mastiffs	48	3,294	60	1,419
Old English Sheepdogs	49	3,178	28	8,332
Newfoundlands	50	3,153	51	2,394

Table 2-1. Dogs Registered by The American Kennel Club, 1982, 1992 (continued)

Breed	1992 Rank	1992 No.	1982 Rank	1982 No.
Wire Fox Terriers *	51	2,889	—	—
Norwegian Elkhounds	52	2,810	43	4,368
Australian Shepherds	53	2,767	—	—
Irish Setters	54	2,718	29	8,183
Silky Terriers	55	2,635	49	2,627
Shiba Inu	56	2,574	—	—
Papillons	57	2,400	74	696
Vizslas	58	2,186	53	1,847
Whippets	59	2,068	61	1,392
Bullmastiffs	60	2,007	71	966
Rhodesian Ridgebacks	61	2,005	63	1,368
Bouviers des Flandres	62	1,994	55	1,632
Basenjis	63	1,925	58	1,517
Italian Greyhounds	64	1,862	81	569
Afghan Hounds	65	1,722	42	4,484
Australian Cattle Dogs	66	1,588	82	558
Bloodhounds	67	1,560	59	1,503
Gordon Setters	68	1,544	69	1,082
Bull Terriers	69	1,505	66	1,162
Bernese Mountain Dogs	70	1,502	86	424
German Wirehaired Pointers	71	1,485	70	1,049
English Cocker Spaniels	72	1,425	62	1,391
Soft-Coated Wheaten Terriers	73	1,407	68	1,111
Borzois	74	1,308	64	1,366
Irish Wolfhounds	75	1,223	67	1,131
Japanese Chin	76	1,217	89	386
Giant Schnauzers	77	1,178	77	634
Smooth Fox Terriers *	78	1,094	—	—
American Staffordshire Terriers	79	1,043	57	1,550
English Setters	80	940	65	1,205
French Bulldogs	81	853	105	182
Portuguese Water Dogs	82	803	—	—
Welsh Terriers	83	787	75	656
Bearded Collies	84	766	73	763
Tibetan Terriers	85	691	84	495
Chinese Cresteds	86	676	—	—
Border Terriers	87	653	97	272
Cardigan Welsh Corgis	88	646	88	393
Belgian Sheepdogs	89	645	78	605
Standard Schnauzers	90	599	76	653
Brussels Griffons	90	599	104	199
Salukis	92	581	78	605
Australian Terriers	93	578	72	774
Belgian Tervuren	94	572	85	446
Pointers	95	564	87	419
Manchester Terriers	96	558	83	519
Kerry Blue Terriers	97	519	80	593
Flat-Coated Retrievers	98	491	95	283
Kuvaszok	99	483	100	235
Belgian Malinois	100	451	120	45

AVMA Center for Information Management

29

Pet Breeds

Table 2-1. Dogs Registered by The American Kennel Club, 1982, 1992 (continued)

Breed	1992 Rank	1992 No.	1982 Rank	1982 No.
Norwich Terriers	101	374	98	243
Tibetan Spaniels	102	371	—	—
Irish Terriers	103	350	93	312
American Water Spaniels	104	347	91	331
Norfolk Terriers	105	334	108	134
Briards	106	321	96	277
Greyhounds	107	275	111	127
Welsh Springer Spaniels	107	275	103	200
Staffordshire Bull Terriers	109	267	99	236
Bedlington Terriers	110	245	90	379
Lakeland Terriers	111	243	101	229
Petits Bassets Griffons Vendens	112	241	—	—
Black and Tan Coonhounds	113	213	94	284
Curly-Coated Retrievers	114	207	119	50
Finnish Spitz	115	204	—	—
Komondorok	116	197	109	128
Affenpinschers	117	191	112	97
Wirehaired Pointing Griffons	118	185	109	128
Pulik	119	175	92	326
Scottish Deerhounds	120	162	106	171
English Toy Spaniels	121	157	118	56
Miniature Bull Terriers	122	131	—	—
Irish Water Spaniels	123	130	114	85
Clumber Spaniels	124	128	115	77
Skye Terriers	125	127	102	223
Dandie Dinmont Terriers	126	118	107	152
Ibizan Hounds	127	114	113	93
Pharaoh Hounds	128	93	—	—
Sealyham Terriers	129	87	116	73
Field Spaniels	130	82	123	27
English Foxhounds	131	73	125	12
Otterhounds	132	67	121	34
Sussex Spaniels	133	51	124	22
American Foxhounds	134	44	117	57
Harriers	135	37	121	34
Fox Terriers *	—	—	47	3,815
Total Registrations		1,438,311		1,037,149

* Wire and Smooth Fox Terriers were registered as one breed prior to March 1, 1985.

Figure 2-1 illustrates the change between 1982 and 1992 in the number of new registrations of dogs of the five most popular breeds.

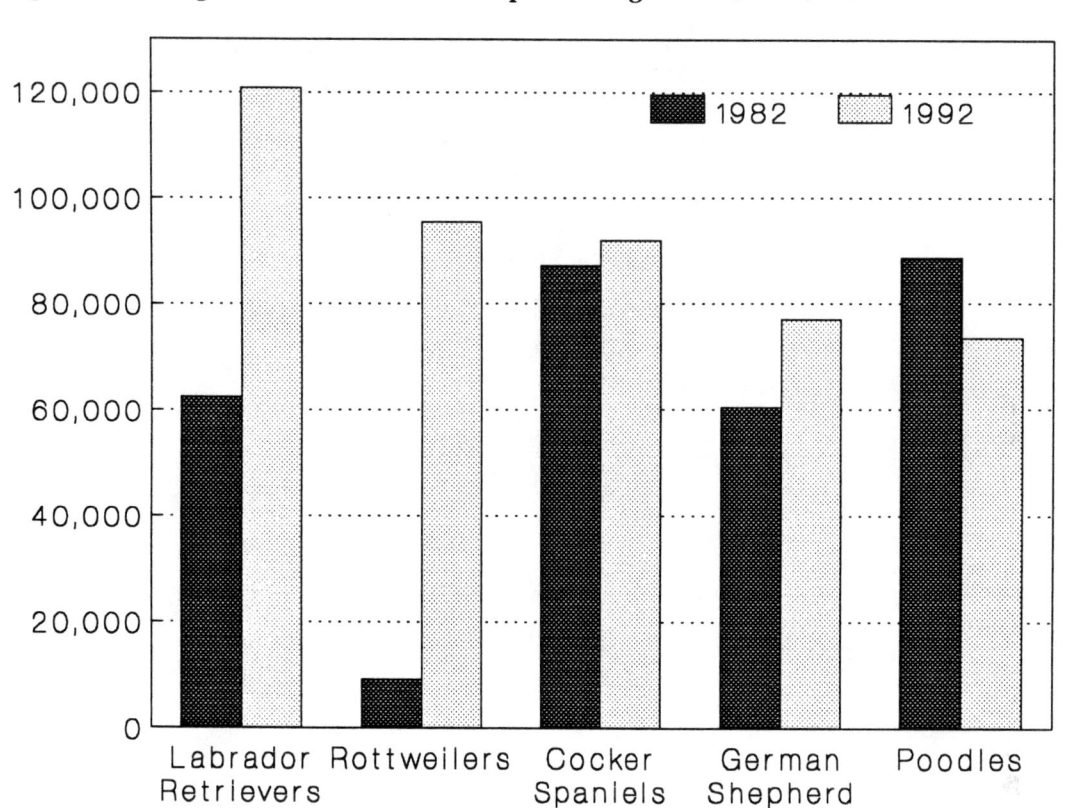

Figure 2-1. Registration Numbers of Top Five Dog Breeds, 1982, 1992

■ CAT BREEDS

There are 39 breeds of cats listed with the Cat Fanciers' Association, Inc., and 73,879 cats were registered during 1992.

Comparing the rank order between 1992 and 1982, four breeds have remained among the top five for number of cats registered. These breeds are the Persian, Maine Coon, Siamese, and Abyssinian. Exotic Shorthairs were the fifth most popular breed, in terms of number of cats registered during 1992, replaced the Burmese among the five most popular breeds.

Persians, with 50,166 cats registered, accounted for 68% of total cat registrations in 1992. The number of Persians registered increased from 31,064 in 1982, and Persians continue to be the most popular breed. The number of Maine Coons registered increased from 1,049 (5th place) in 1982 to 3,121 (2nd place) in 1992. Only 3,047 Siamese were registered in 1992 compared with 3,570 in 1982, and Siamese dropped in rank from second to third. There was a decrease in the number of registered Abyssinians between 1982 and 1992, resulting in a drop from third place (2,124) to fourth place (2,407). The Exotic Shorthair breed jumped in rank from fourteenth place, with 353 registrations in 1982, to fifth place, with 1,355 registrations in 1992.

The rank order by number of cats registered during 1992 are listed in Table 2-2.

Table 2-2. Cats Registered by Cat Fanciers' Association, 1982, 1992

Breeds	1992 Rank	1992 No.	1982 Rank	1982 No.
Persian	1	50,166	1	31,064
Maine Coon	2	3,121	5	1,049
Siamese	3	3,047	2	3,570
Abyssinian	4	2,407	3	2,124
Exotic Shorthair	5	1,355	14	353
American Shorthair	6	1,233	7	766
Scottish Fold	7	1,217	15	332
Oriental Shorthair	8	1,209	10	512
Birman	9	980	13	396
Burmese	10	970	4	1,323
Ocicat	11	872	27	56
Tonkinese	12	739	17	189
Cornish Rex	13	706	9	570
Somali	14	643	16	287
Colorpoint Shorthair	15	636	6	935
Devon Rex	16	557	23	71
Manx	17	549	8	639
Russian Blue	18	455	12	457
Balinese	19	354	11	495
British Shorthair	20	328	18	135
Egyptian Mau	21	307	21	96
Japanese Bobtail	22	266	24	68
Javanese	23	220	22	81
Norweigan Forest Cat *	24	216	—	—
Chartreux	25	203	30	24
Highland Fold *	26	145	—	—
Cymric	27	135	28	35
Korat	28	123	20	118
Turkish Angora	29	113	19	125
Bombay	30	93	25	57
Singapura	31	89	31	20
Turkish Van *	32	85	—	—
American Curl Longhair *	33	83	—	—
Havana Brown	34	75	25	57
American Curl Shorthair *	35	65	—	—
Selkirk Rex *	36	57	—	—
American Wirehair	37	37	29	25
Oriental Longhair *	38	23	—	—
Total Registrations		73,879		46,029

* Not accepted for registration in 1982.

Pet Breeds

Changes between 1982 and 1992 in the number of new registrations of cats of the five most popular breeds are shown in Figure 2-2.

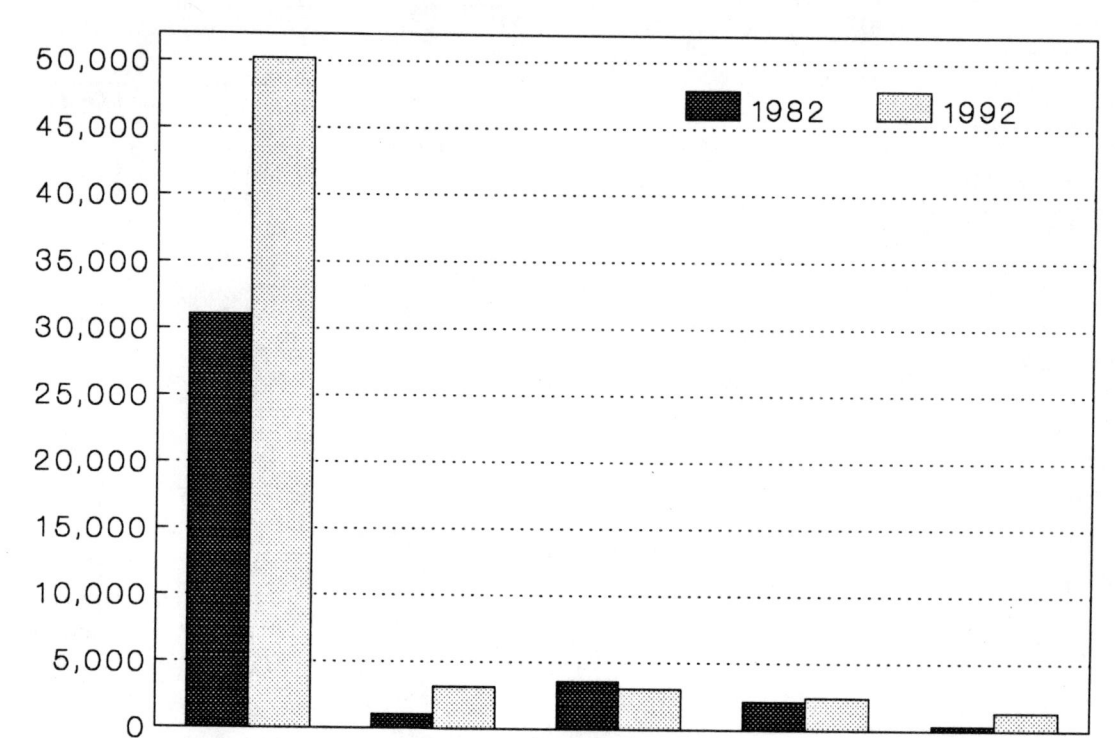

Figure 2-3. Registration Numbers of Top Five Cat Breeds, 1982, 1992

CHAPTER 3

Demographics of Pet Ownership

■ PET OWNERSHIP DEMOGRAPHICS

Demographic characteristics influence whether a household will own a pet. Four demographic variables that can be used to compare households that own a pet with households that don't own a pet are life-stage, income, size of household, and home ownership.

Household life-stage is a method used to classify households on the basis of family composition. The following life-stage categories of households are defined.

> Young Singles: 1-member, less than 35 years old;
> Middle Singles: 1-member, between 35 and 65 years old;
> Older Singles: 1-member, more than 65 years old;
> Young Couple: multi-members, age of household head under 45, no children present;
> Working Older Couple: multi-members, age of head over 45, working, no children present;
> Retired Older Couple: multi-members, age of head over 45, not working, no children present;
> Young Parent: multi-members, age of head under 45, youngest child under 6 years old;
> Middle Parent: multi-members, age of head under 45, youngest child 6 or more years old;
> Older Parent: multi-members, age of head 45 or older, child of any age at home
> Other: (Roommates) multi-members, nonrelatives, 18 years and over, of same sex.

Pet-owning households are more likely to be parent households with children than single-member households (Table 3-1). Approximately 72% of parent households own a pet, and less than 39% of single-member households own a pet (Figure 3-1).

Pet Demographics

Table 3-1. Demographics of Pet Ownership, by Life-stage, 1991

Life-stage	Households That Own a Pet (Pct.)	Households That Don't Own a Pet (Pct.)
Young singles	48.2	51.8
Middle singles	43.0	57.0
Older singles	29.2	70.8
Young couple	70.4	29.6
Working older couple	55.4	44.6
Retired older couple	41.1	58.9
Young parents	67.4	32.6
Middle parents	78.7	21.3
Older parents	71.3	28.7
Others	70.7	29.3

Figure 3-1. Demographics of Pet Ownership, by Life-stage, 1991

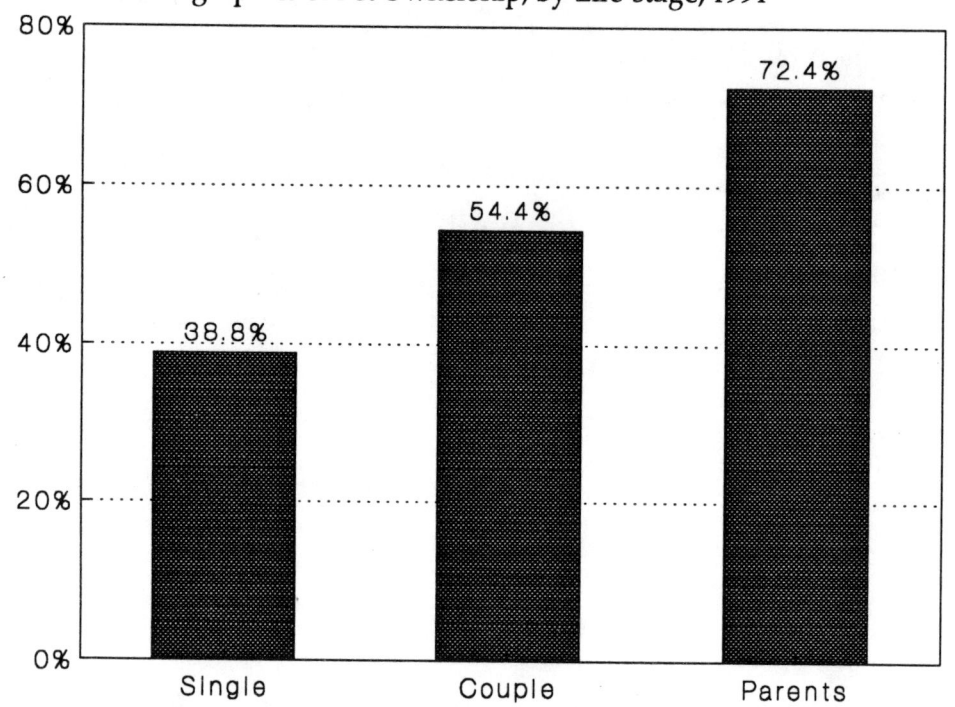

Single	Couple	Parents
38.8%	54.4%	72.4%

Pet Demographics

The percentage of households that own a pet increases as household income increases (Table 3-2). Specifically, 47% of housholds with household income less than $12,500 own a pet; 54% of households with incomes between $12,500 and $24,999 own a pet; and at least 60% of households with incomes greater than $25,000 own a pet.

Table 3-2. Demographics of Pet Ownership, by Household Income, 1991

Household Income	Households That Own a Pet (Pct.)	Households That Don't Own a Pet (Pct.)
Under $12,500	47.4	52.6
$12,500 to $24,999	54.2	45.8
$25,000 to $39,999	60.3	39.7
$40,000 to $59,999	63.1	36.9
$60,000 and over	64.2	35.8

Household size (ie, number of members of a household) is directly related to pet ownership. Pets are owned by 38% of 1-member households, 55% of 2-member households, 70% of 3-member households, and 75% of households with 4 or more members (Table 3-3). Figure 3-2 on the following page graphically shows this trend.

Table 3-3. Demographics of Pet Ownership, by Household Size, 1991

Household Size	Households That Own a Pet (Pct.)	Households That Don't Own a Pet (Pct.)
1 member	38.8	61.2
2 members	55.2	44.8
3 members	70.0	30.0
4 members	74.7	25.3
5 or more members	76.0	24.0

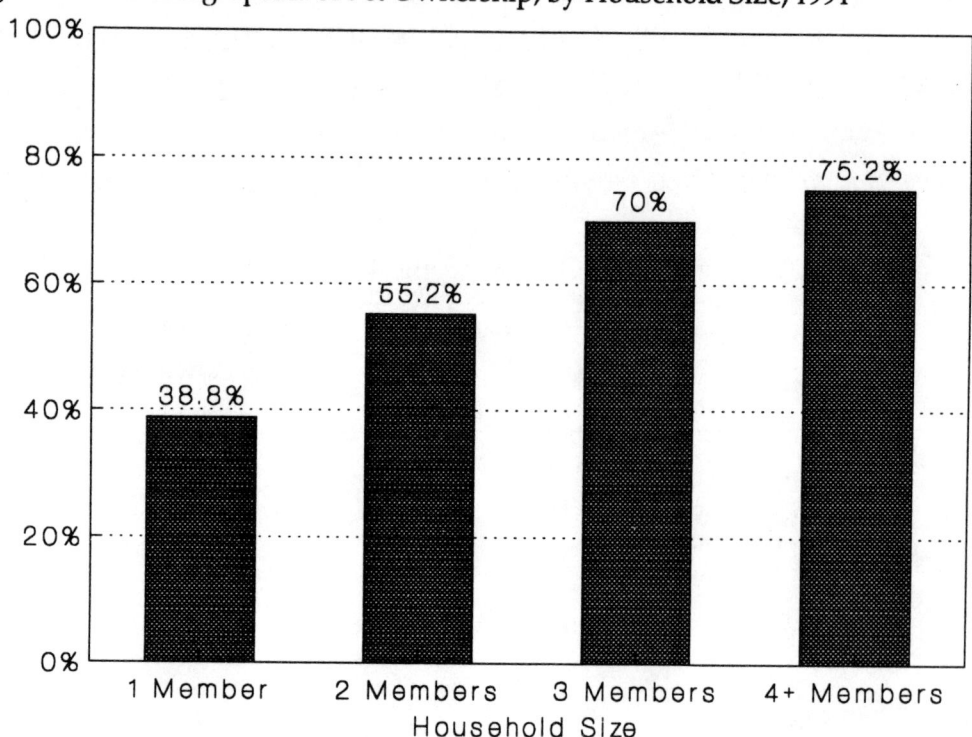

Figure 3-2. Demographics of Pet Ownership, by Household Size, 1991

Household Size	Percentage
1 Member	38.8%
2 Members	55.2%
3 Members	70%
4+ Members	75.2%

Pet ownership is more common among households that own their home (Table 3-4). Sixty percent of home owners own a pet, compared with 50% of renters.

Table 3-4. Demographics of Pet Ownership, by Home Ownership, 1991

Home Ownership	Households That Own a Pet (Pct.)	Households That Don't Own a Pet (Pct.)
Own	60.7	39.3
Rent	49.8	50.2
Other*	59.9	40.1
No answer	41.9	58.1

*Other = miscellaneous, e.g. living with relatives

■ DOG OWNERSHIP DEMOGRAPHICS

Dog ownership can be compared among households according to life-stage characteristics. This method classifies households on the basis of family composition (Table 3-5).

Table 3-5. Demographics of Dog Ownership, by Life-stage, 1991

Life-stage	Households That Own a Dog (Pct.)	Households That Don't Own a Dog (Pct.)
Young singles	20.5	79.5
Middle singles	22.5	77.5
Older singles	16.2	83.8
Young couple	41.4	58.6
Working older couple	35.7	64.3
Retired older couple	26.8	73.2
Young parents	43.2	56.8
Middle parents	54.3	45.7
Older parents	49.1	50.9
Others	42.9	57.1

The percentage of households is higher for young, middle-aged, or older parents than for other life-stage groups (Figure 3-3). Approximately 49% of older parent households own dogs; 54% of middle-aged parent households own dogs; and 43% of young parent households own dogs.

Pet Demographics

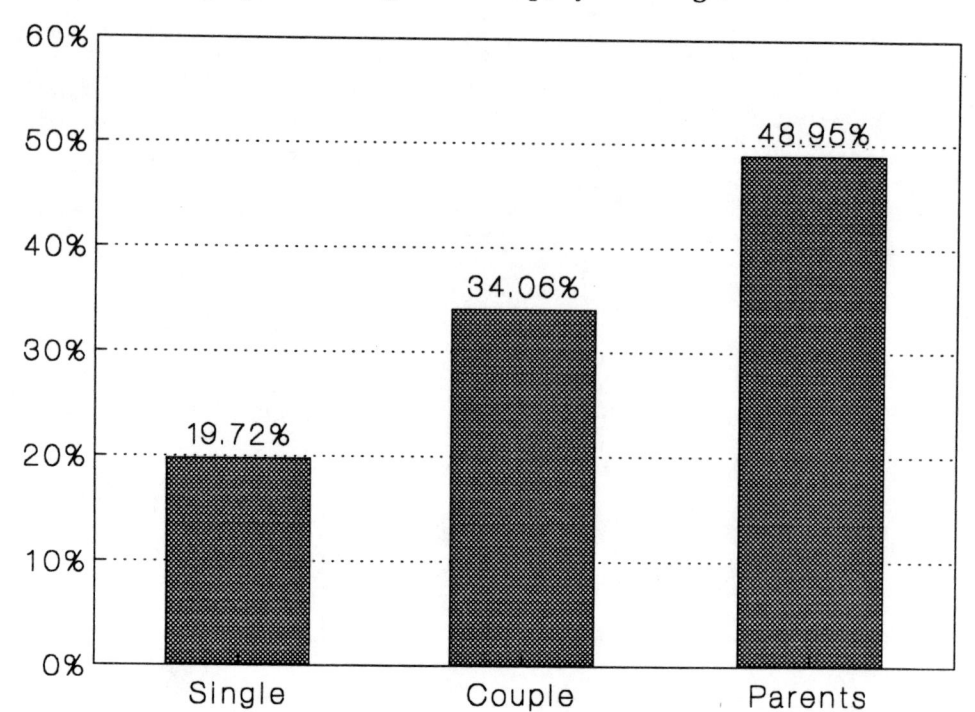

Figure 3-3. Demographics of Dog Ownership, by Life-stage, 1991

Life-stage	Percentage
Single	19.72%
Couple	34.06%
Parents	48.95%

The percentage of households owning a dog increases with increasing household income. For example, 29% of households with incomes under $12,500 own dogs, compared with 41% of households with incomes over $60,000 (Table 3-6).

Table 3-6. Demographics of Dog Ownership, by Household Income, 1991

Household Income	Households That Own a Dog (Pct.)	Households That Don't Own a Dog (Pct.)
Under $12,500	29.2	70.8
$12,500 to $24,999	33.9	66.1
$25,000 to $39,999	38.6	61.4
$40,000 to $59,999	39.9	60.1
$60,000 and over	40.7	59.3

Table 3-7. Demographics of Dog Ownership, by Household Size, 1991

Household Size	Households That Own a Dog (Pct.)	Households That Don't Own a Dog (Pct.)
1 member	19.7	80.3
2 members	33.9	66.1
3 members	45.9	54.1
4 members	52.4	47.6
5 or more members	53.8	46.2

Larger households are more likely to own dogs (Table 3-7). Twenty percent of single-member households own dogs, compared with 54% of 5-or-more-member households that own dogs.

Figure 3-4. Demographics of Dog Ownership, by Household Size, 1991

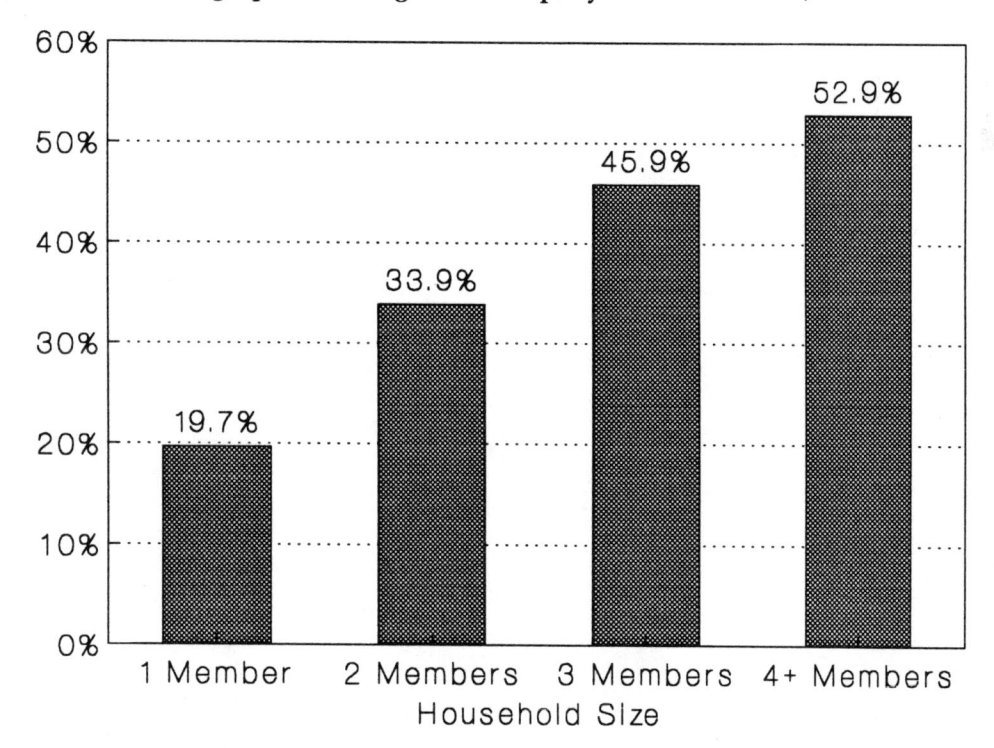

Pet Demographics

Households that own their home are more likely to own a dog than households that rent their home. Specifically, 41% of home owners have dogs compared with 24% of renters (Table 3-8).

Table 3-8.   Demographics of Dog Ownership, by Home Ownership, 1991

Home Ownership	Households That Own a Dog (Pct.)	Households That Don't Own a Dog (Pct.)
Own	40.7	59.3
Rent	23.6	76.4
Other*	38.4	61.6

*Other = miscellaneous, e.g. living with relatives

■ CAT OWNERSHIP DEMOGRAPHICS

According to life-stage characteristics of US households, cat ownership is more common among young couples (40.3%), young parents (34.2%), middle-aged parents (42.6%), and older parent households (39.1%) (Table 3-9).

Table 3-9. Demographics of Cat Ownership, by Life-stage, 1991

Life-stage	Households That Own a Cat (Pct.)	Households That Don't Own a Cat (Pct.)
Young singles	26.8	73.2
Middle singles	24.0	76.0
Older singles	14.4	85.6
Young couple	40.3	59.7
Working older couple	28.5	71.5
Retired older couple	19.8	80.2
Young parents	34.2	65.8
Middle parents	42.6	57.4
Older parents	39.1	60.9
Others	39.8	60.2

Only 14.4% of older single households and 19.8% of retired, older couples own cats, as illustrated in Figure 3-5 on the next page.

Pet Demographics

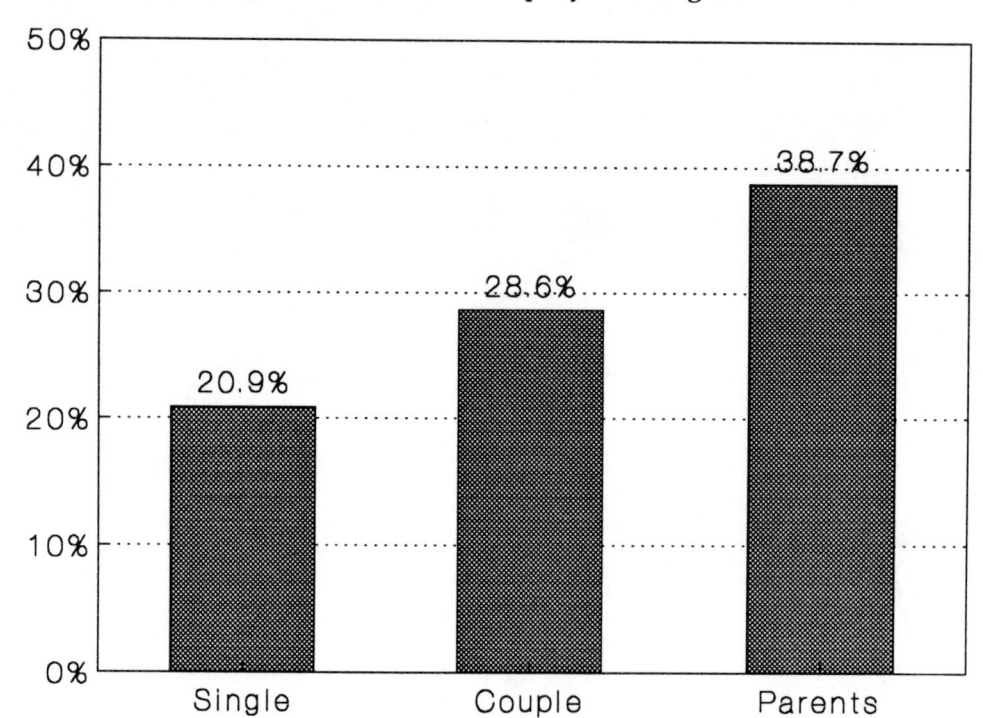

Figure 3-5.   Demographics of Cat Ownership, by Life-stage, 1991

[Bar chart showing: Single 20.9%, Couple 28.6%, Parents 38.7%]

A larger percentage of high income households than low income households own cats. Approximately 25% of households with incomes under $12,500 own cats compared with 34% of households with incomes over $60,000 that own cats. In general, data in Table 3-10 show a direct relationship between increased income and cat ownership.

Table 3-10.   Demographics of Cat Ownership, by Household Income, 1991

Household Income	Households That Own a Cat (Pct.)	Households That Own a Cat (Pct.)
Under $12,500	24.7	75.3
$12,500 to $24,999	29.7	70.3
$25,000 to $39,999	32.1	67.9
$40,000 to $59,999	33.5	66.5
$60,000 and over	34.0	66.0

Table 3-11. Demographics of Cat Ownership, by Household Size, 1991

Household Size	Households That Own a Cat (Pct.)	Households That Don't Own a Cat (Pct.)
1 member	20.9	79.1
2 members	29.2	70.8
3 members	37.3	62.7
4 members	39.4	60.6
5 or more members	41.0	59.0

Similar to household income, household size is positively related with percentage of households that own cats (Table 3-11). For example, 21% of 1-member households own cats, compared with 41% of 5-or-more-member households.

Figure 3-6. Demographics of Cat Ownership, by Household Size, 1991

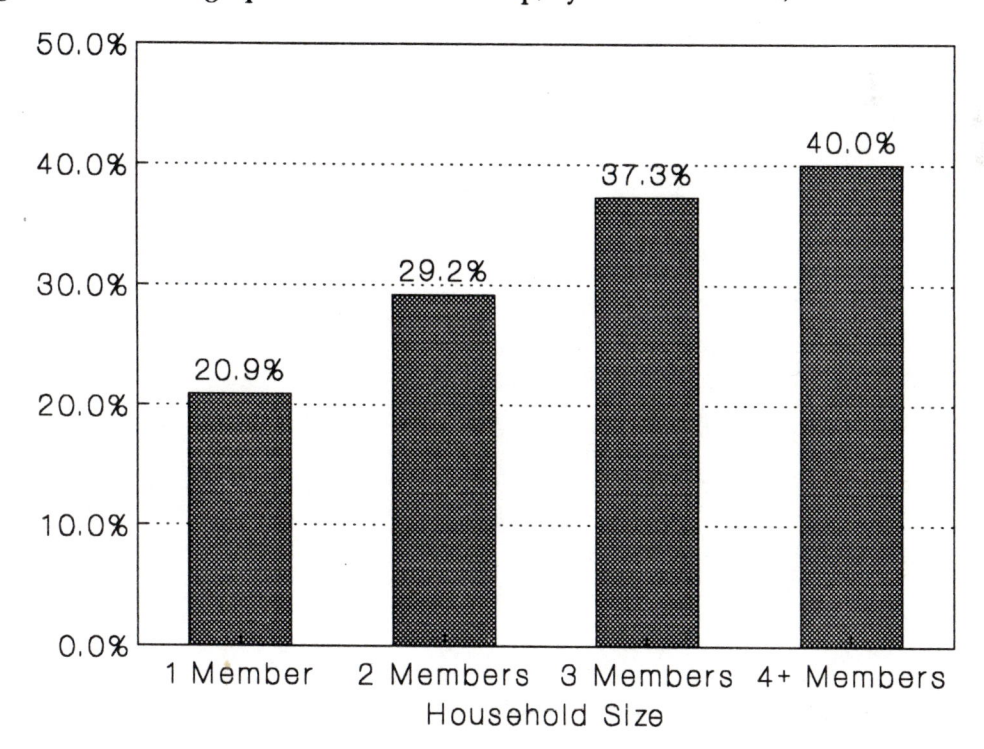

Pet Demographics

The percentage of home owners and of renters that own cats are similar (Table 3-12). Specifically, 31.8% of home owners own cats, compared with 28.4% of renters.

Table 3-12. Demographics of Cat Ownership, by Home Ownership, 1991

Home Ownership	Households That Own a Cat (Pct.)	Households That Don't Own a Cat (Pct.)
Own	31.8	68.2
Rent	28.4	71.6
Other*	32.3	67.7

*Other = miscellaneous, e.g. living with relatives

■ BIRD DEMOGRAPHICS

On the basis of life-stage characteristics, parent households are the most likely to own pet birds. Middle-aged parent households are more likely to own pet birds than are young parent or older parent households. Between 6% and 7% of young couples, young parents, and older parent households also own pet birds (Table 3-13).

Table 3-13. Demographics of Bird Ownership, by Life-stage, 1991

Life-stage	Households That Own a Bird (Pct.)	Households That Don't Own a Bird (Pct.)
Young singles	4.8	95.2
Middle singles	3.9	96.1
Older singles	2.2	97.8
Young couple	6.5	93.5
Working older couple	4.2	95.8
Retired older couple	2.9	97.1
Young parents	6.7	93.3
Middle parents	10.2	89.8
Older parents	7.8	92.2
Others	6.3	93.7

Figure 3-7 on the next page illustrates the demographics of bird ownership in single, couple, and parent households.

Pet Demographics

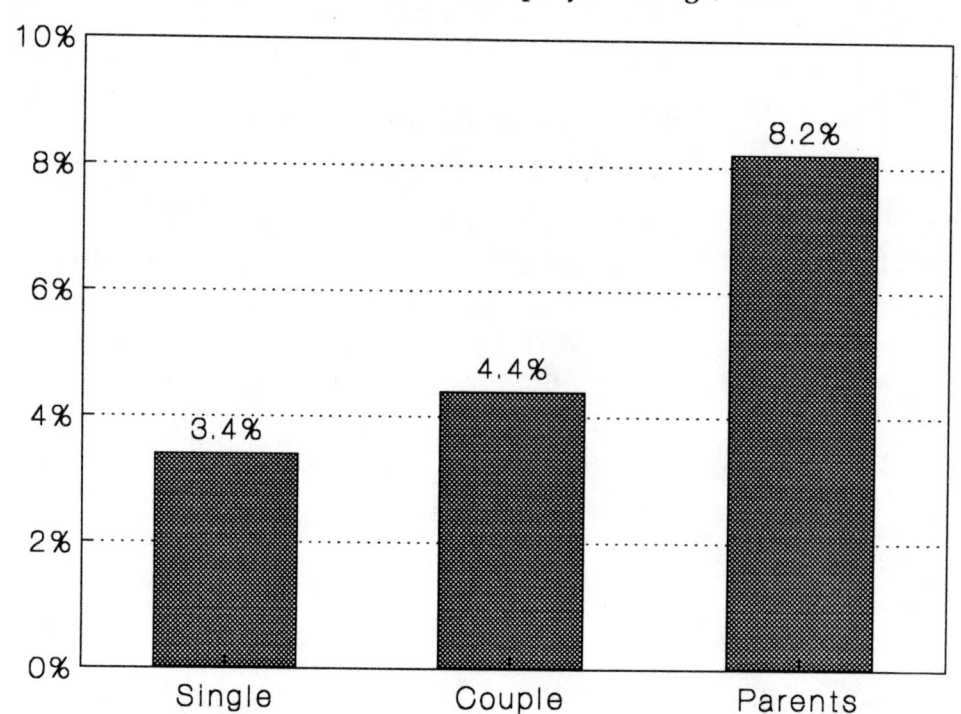

Figure 3-7. Demographics of Bird Ownership, by Life-stage, 1991

- Single: 3.4%
- Couple: 4.4%
- Parents: 8.2%

Percentage of households owning a bird varies only slightly with household income. More middle-income households own birds. To illustrate, 6.1% of households in the $25,000 to $39,999 and with $40,000 to $59,000 income groups own birds (Table 3-14). This compares with 5.6% of households in the $60,000 and over group, and the $12,500 to $24,999 group.

Table 3-14. Demographics of Bird Ownership, by Household Income, 1991

Household Income	Households That Own a Bird (Pct.)	Households That Don't Own a Bird (Pct.)
Under $12,500	5.2	94.8
$12,500 to $24,999	5.6	94.4
$25,000 to $39,999	6.1	93.9
$40,000 to $59,999	6.1	93.9
$60,000 and over	5.6	94.4

Pet Demographics

Table 3-15. Demographics of Bird Ownership, by Household Size, 1991

Household Size	Households That Own a Bird (Pct.)	Households That Don't Own a Bird (Pct.)
1 member	3.4	96.6
2 members	4.5	95.5
3 members	6.9	93.1
4 members	8.6	91.4
5 or more members	10.7	89.3

Increases in household size are associated with an increased likelihood of bird ownership (Table 3-15). Eleven percent of 5-or-more-member households own birds, compared with 3.4% of 1-member households. Figure 3-8 graphically illustrates the strong relationship between household size and bird ownership.

Figure 3-8. Demographics of Bird Ownership, by Household Size, 1991

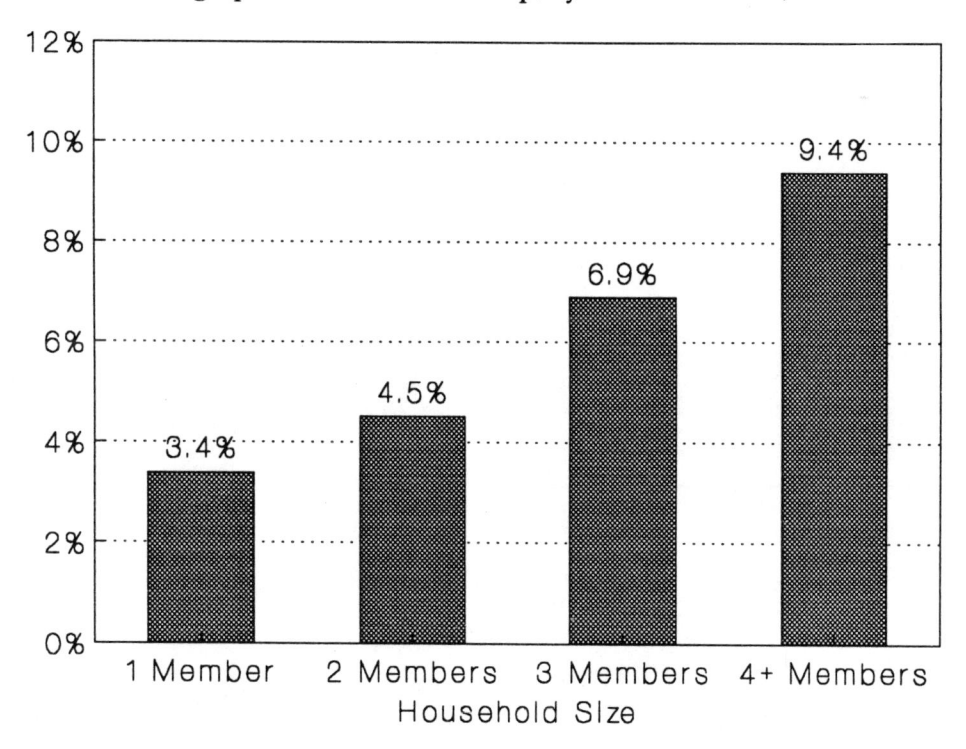

Household Size	Percent
1 Member	3.4%
2 Members	4.5%
3 Members	6.9%
4+ Members	9.4%

AVMA Center for Information Management

Pet Demographics

Renters are slightly more likely to own birds than are home owners (Table 3-16). Specifically, 6.4% of renters own birds, compared with 5.5% of home owners.

Table 3-16. Demographics of Bird Ownership, by Home Ownership, 1991

Home Ownership	Households That Own a Bird (Pct.)	Households That Don't Own a Bird (Pct.)
Own	5.5	94.5
Rent	6.4	93.6
Other*	7.0	93.0

*Other = miscellaneous, e.g. living with relatives

■ HORSE OWNERSHIP DEMOGRAPHICS

On the basis of life-stage characteristics of US households, young couple, young parent, middle parent, and older parent households are the most likely to own horses; however the percentages of households that own horses are relatively small (Table 3-17).

Table 3-17. Demographics of Horse Ownership, by Life-stage, 1991

Life-stage	Households That Own a Horse (Pct.)	Households That Don't Own a Horse (Pct.)
Young singles	1.2	98.8
Middle singles	0.9	99.1
Older singles	0.3	99.7
Young couple	2.6	97.4
Working older couple	2.5	97.5
Retired older couple	1.5	98.5
Young parents	2.6	97.4
Middle parents	2.9	97.1
Older parents	2.8	97.2
Others	1.3	98.7

To summarize, 0.7% of single households, 2.2% of couple households, and 2.8% of parent households own horses (Figure 3-9).

Pet Demographics

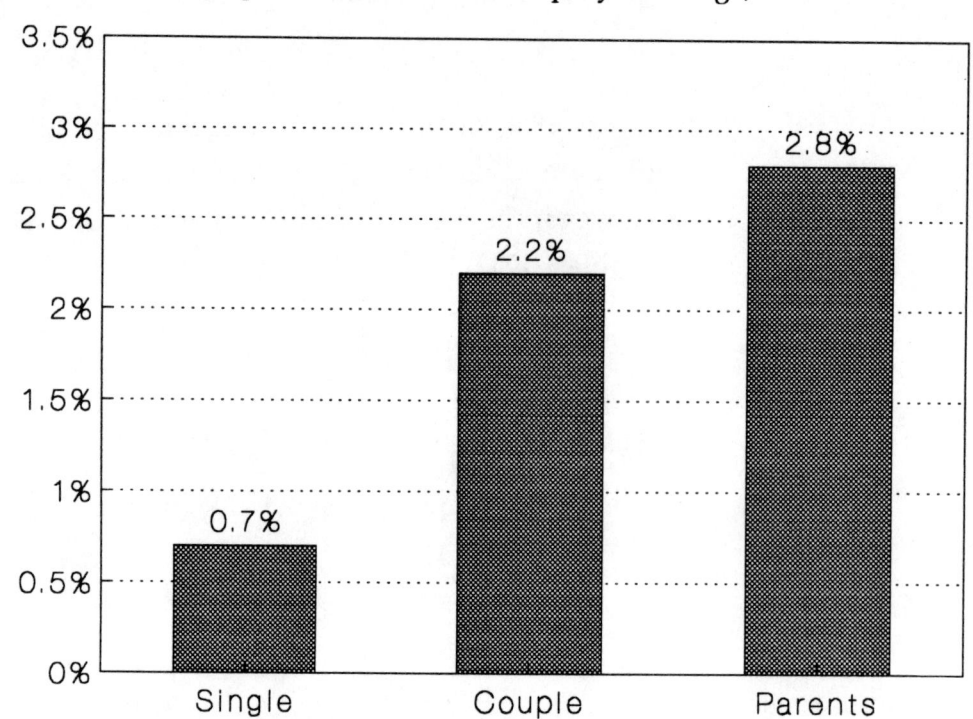

Figure 3-9. Demographics of Horse Ownership, by Life-stage, 1991

Life-stage	Percentage
Single	0.7%
Couple	2.2%
Parents	2.8%

Horse ownership is associated with household income. Specifically, 1.0% of households with incomes under $12,500 own a horse, compared with 2.6% of households with incomes over $60,000 (Table 3-18).

Table 3-18. Demographics of Horse Ownership, by Household Income, 1991

Household Income	Households That Own a Horse (Pct.)	Households That Don't Own a Horse (Pct.)
Under $12,500	1.0	99.0
$12,500 to $24,999	2.1	97.9
$25,000 to $39,999	2.2	97.8
$40,000 to $59,999	2.2	97.8
$60,000 and over	2.6	97.4

Table 3-19. Demographics of Horse Ownership, by Household Size, 1991

Household Size	Households That Own a Horse (Pct.)	Households That Don't Own a Horse (Pct.)
1 member	0.7	99.3
2 members	2.0	98.0
3 members	2.5	97.5
4 members	3.1	96.9
5 or more members	3.5	96.5

Increases in household size are associated with small increases in the percentage of households that own horses (Table 3-19). For example, 0.7% of 1-member households own horses, compared with 3.5% of 5-or-more-member households.

Figure 3-10. Demographics of Horse Ownership, by Household Size, 1991

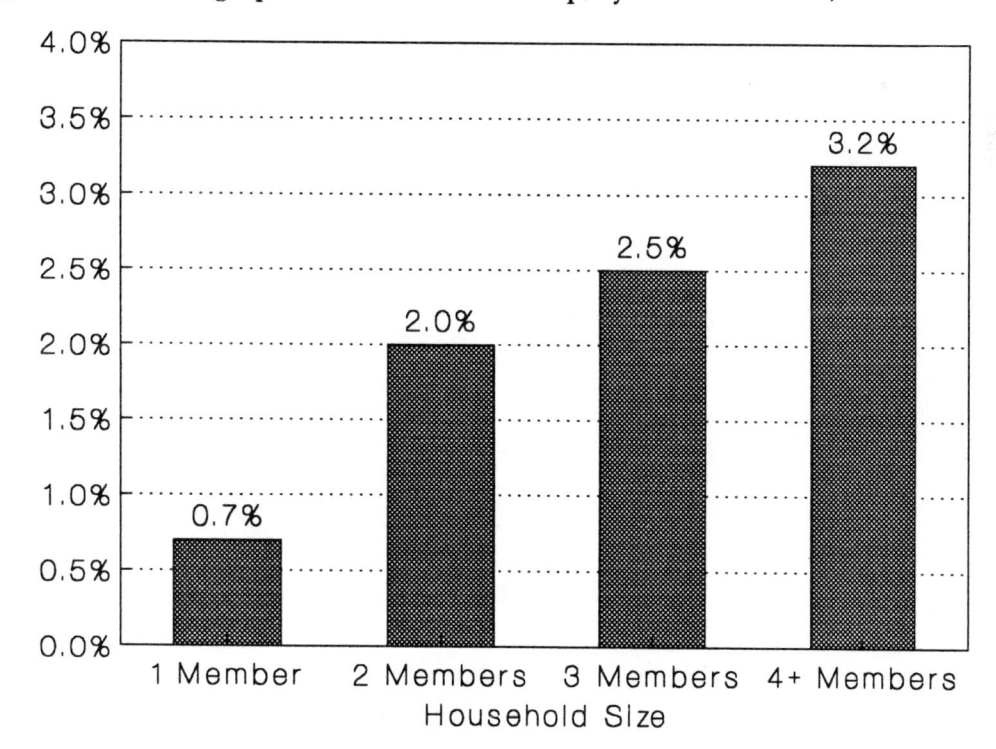

Household Size	Percent
1 Member	0.7%
2 Members	2.0%
3 Members	2.5%
4+ Members	3.2%

Pet Demographics

Home owners are more likely to own horses than are renters. One percent of households renting their home own a horse; 2.3% of households that own their home own a horse (Table 3-20).

Table 3-20. Demographics of Horse Ownership, by Home Ownership, 1991

Home Ownership	Households That Own a Horse (Pct.)	Households That Don't Own a Horse (Pct.)
Own	2.3	97.7
Rent	1.0	99.0
Other*	5.5	94.5

*Other = miscellaneous, e.g. living with relatives

CHAPTER 4

Profiles of Pet-Owning Households

■ PROFILES OF PET-OWNING HOUSEHOLDS

Demographic profiles can help determine the characteristics of the average pet-owning household. Eight profiles used are life-stage, household income, size of household, home ownership, type of residence, population density, education of the male head of the household, and education of the female head of the household.

Household life-stage is a method used to classify households on the basis of family composition. The following life-stage categories of households are defined.

> Young Singles: 1-member, less than 35 years old;
> Middle Singles: 1-member, between 35 and 65 years old;
> Older Singles: 1-member, more than 65 years old;
> Young Couple: multi-members, age of household head under 45, no children present;
> Working Older Couple: multi-members, age of head over 45, working, no children present;
> Retired Older Couple: multi-members, age of head over 45, not working, no children present;
> Young Parent: multi-members, age of head under 45, youngest child under 6 years old;
> Middle Parent: multi-members, age of head under 45, youngest child 6 or more years old;
> Older Parent: multi-members, age of head 45 or older, child of any age at home;
> Other: (Roommates) multi-members, nonrelatives, 18 years and over, of same sex.

Comparing the demographic profile of pet-owning households with that of all households, pet-owning households are more likely to be parent households. To illustrate, 50.4% of pet-owning households are parent households compared with 40.3% of all households. Seventeen percent of pet-owning households are singles compared with 26% of all households (Table 4-1).

Figure 4-1 on the following page graphically contrasts the profile, by life-stage groups, of pet-owning households with the profile of all households.

Pet Profiles

Table 4-1. Profile of Pet-Owning Households, by Life-stage, 1991

Life-stage	% All HH*	% Pet HH	% Dog HH	% Cat HH	% Bird HH	% Horse HH
Young singles	5.2	4.3	2.9	4.5	4.3	3.0
Middle singles	10.9	8.1	6.7	8.5	7.5	5.0
Older singles	9.8	4.9	4.3	4.6	3.8	1.4
Young couple	8.7	10.5	9.8	11.3	9.9	11.2
Working older couple	12.0	11.4	11.7	11.0	8.8	14.8
Retired older couple	11.4	8.1	8.4	7.3	5.7	8.5
Young parents	12.6	14.6	14.9	13.9	14.8	16.1
Middle parents	12.9	17.5	19.2	17.8	23.0	18.4
Older parents	14.8	18.3	20.0	18.8	20.3	20.4
Others	1.8	2.1	2.1	2.3	1.9	1.2
Total	100%	100%	100%	100%	100%	100%

*HH = Households

Figure 4-1. Profile of Pet-Owning Households, by Life-stage, 1991

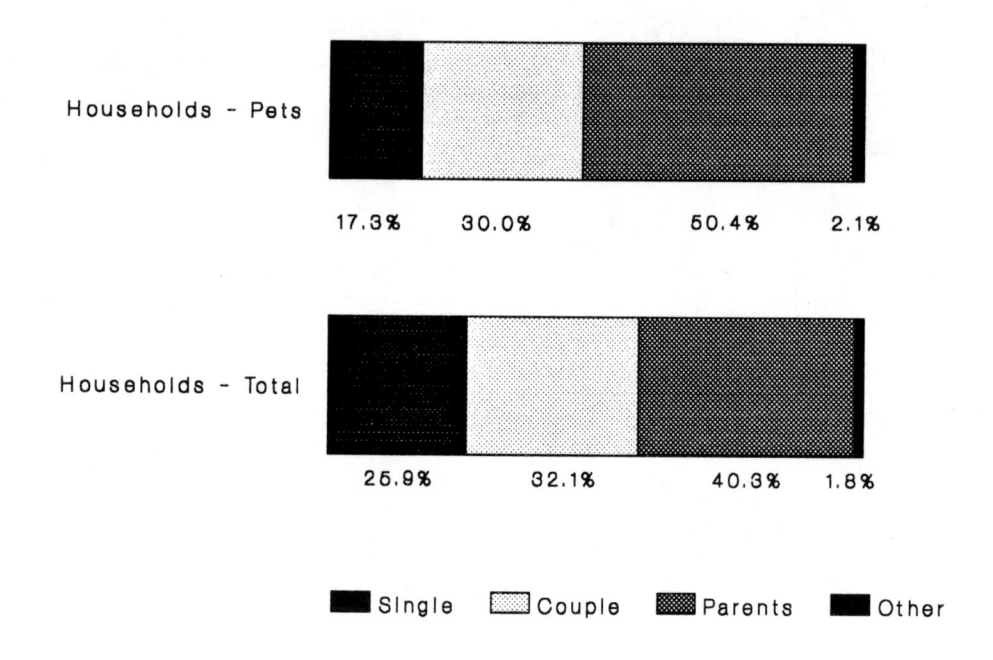

Households - Pets: 17.3% Single, 30.0% Couple, 50.4% Parents, 2.1% Other

Households - Total: 25.9% Single, 32.1% Couple, 40.3% Parents, 1.8% Other

■ Single   □ Couple   ▨ Parents   ■ Other

A slight difference is found between household income of pet-owning households and that of all households. As shown in Table 4-2, a higher percentage of pet-owning households are in the higher income brackets. Specifically 65.2% of pet-owning households have annual incomes over $25,000 compared with 60.6% of all households.

Table 4-2. Profile of Pet-Owning Households, by Household Income, 1991

Annual Income	% All HH*	% Pet HH	%Dog HH	%Cat HH	%Bird HH	%Horse HH
Under $12,500	18.7	15.0	14.6	14.6	16.6	9.2
$12,500 to $24,999	20.7	19.9	19.7	20.4	20.7	21.5
$25,000 to $39,999	22.4	23.5	23.8	23.5	23.9	24.8
$40,000 to $59,999	20.0	21.8	21.8	21.7	21.2	21.9
$60,000 and over	18.2	19.9	20.0	19.8	17.7	22.6
Total	100%	100%	100%	100%	100%	100%

*HH = Households

Pet-owning households tend to be larger-sized households. Only 17.4% of pet-owning households are 1-member households. By comparison, 25% of all households were 1-member households (Table 4-3). Also, 29.5% of pet-owning households are 4-or-more-member households. By comparison, 25.4% of all households in the US were 4-or-more-member households. Figure 4-2 on the following page graphically compares the profile, according to size of household, of pet-owning households with the profile of all US households.

Pet Profiles

Table 4-3. Profile of Pet-Owning Households, by Household Size, 1991

Household Size	% All HH*	% Pet HH	% Dog HH	% Cat HH	% Bird HH	% Horse HH
1 member	24.7	17.4	14.0	17.6	15.6	9.5
2 members	32.6	33.4	32.5	33.2	27.5	34.4
3 members	17.3	19.7	20.5	19.7	19.6	20.2
4 members	15.5	18.3	20.4	18.1	21.4	21.3
5 or more members	9.9	11.2	12.6	11.3	15.9	14.6
Total	100%	100%	100%	100%	100%	100%

*HH = Households

Figure 4-2. Profile of Pet-Owning Households, by Household Size, 1991

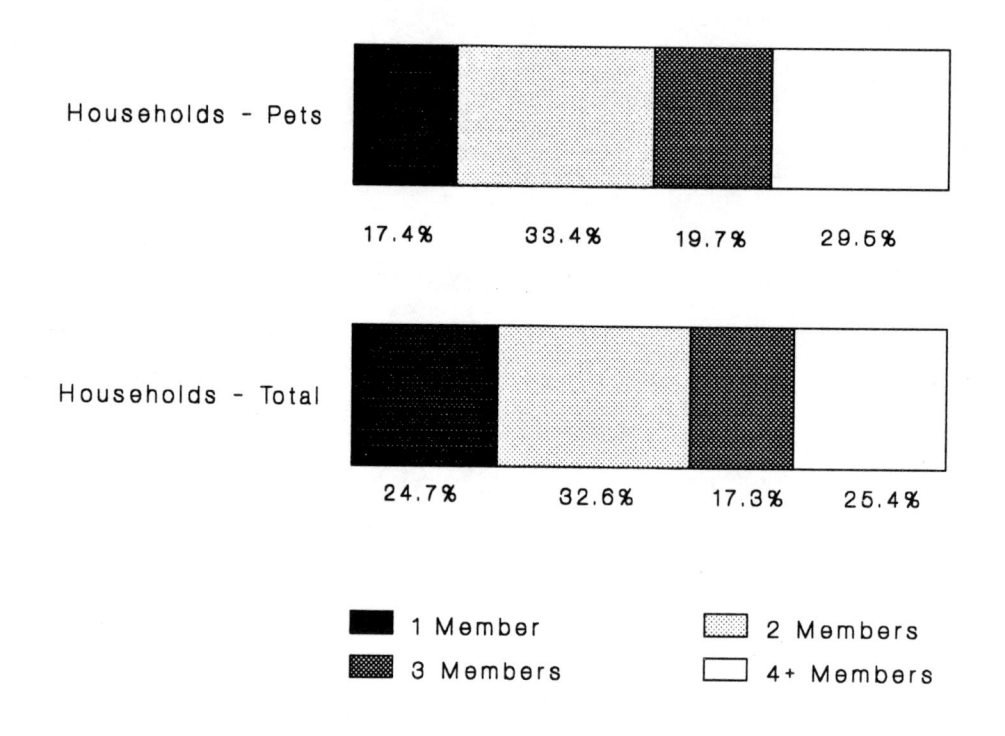

Households - Pets: 17.4% 33.4% 19.7% 29.5%

Households - Total: 24.7% 32.6% 17.3% 25.4%

■ 1 Member ▨ 2 Members
▨ 3 Members □ 4+ Members

AVMA Center for Information Management

A larger percentage of pet-owning households, than of all US households, own their home. Seventy-six percent of companion animal owners own their home; whereas, only 73% of all households own their home (Table 4-4). A smaller percentage of pet-owning households, than of all US households, rent their home.

Table 4-4. Profile of Pet-Owning Households, by Home Ownership, 1991

Home Ownership	% All HH*	% Pet HH	% Dog HH	% Cat HH	% Bird HH	% Horse HH
Own	72.7	76.2	80.9	74.8	69.4	82.4
Rent	21.2	18.2	13.7	19.5	23.9	10.8
Other**	3.7	3.8	3.9	3.9	4.5	5.1
Did not specify	2.5	1.8	1.5	1.9	2.2	1.7
Total	100%	100%	100%	100%	100%	100%

*HH = Households   **Other = miscellaneous, e.g. living with relatives

A direct correlation between home ownership and type of residence can be seen for pet-owning households. A large number of pet-owning households own, rather than rent, their homes. Approximately 79% of pet-owning households live in a house, whereas, 72% of all households live in a house (Table 4-5). Only 8% of pet-owning households live in an apartment, but 13.1% of all households live in an apartment.

Table 4-5. Profile of Pet-Owning Households, by Type of Residence, 1991

Type of Residence	% All HH*	% Pet HH	% Dog HH	% Cat HH	% Bird HH	% Horse HH
House	72.4	78.6	84.0	77.3	72.9	84.6
Apartment	13.1	8.0	3.8	8.8	11.3	2.0
Mobile home	6.1	6.6	7.2	6.7	6.9	10.1
Condominium	3.5	2.2	1.2	2.4	3.1	0.5
Duplex	2.5	2.4	1.9	2.5	3.1	1.0
Other	1.2	1.0	0.7	1.0	1.0	0.5
Did not specify	1.4	1.3	1.3	1.3	1.6	1.3
Total	100%	100%	100%	100%	100%	100%

*HH = Households

Pet Profiles

Small differences between pet-owning households and all households could be found when population density was analyzed. These differences were apparent for households located in areas with populations less than 100,000 and for households located in areas with populations more than 2,000,000. Specifically, 25.7% of pet-owning households live in areas with a population of 100,000 or less and 37.4% live in areas with a population of 2,000,000 or more. This compares with the finding that 23.9% of all households live in areas with a population of 100,000 or less and 39.6% of all households live in areas with a population of 2,000,000 or more (Table 4-6).

Table 4-6. Profile of Pet-Owning Households, by Population Density, 1991

Population	% All HH*	% Pet HH	% Dog HH	% Cat HH	% Bird HH	% Horse HH
100,000	23.9	25.7	28.7	27.8	22.6	47.4
100,000 to 499,999	16.0	16.5	17.0	15.8	16.0	16.4
500,000 to 1,999,999	20.5	20.5	19.9	20.2	19.4	15.5
2,000,000 and over	39.6	37.4	34.4	36.3	42.0	20.7
Total	100%	100%	100%	100%	100%	100%

*HH = Households

Regarding education level of the male and female head of household, there are slight differences between pet-owning households and all households, as listed in Table 4-7 and Table 4-8 on the following page.

Table 4-7. Profile of Pet-Owning Households, by Education Level of the Male Head of Household, 1991

Education	% All HH*	% Pet HH	% Dog HH	% Cat HH	% Bird HH	% Horse HH
High school or less	28.4	30.3	34.0	29.3	31.7	39.6
Attended college	19.3	21.0	21.9	20.6	22.1	23.3
Graduated college	11.9	11.9	11.2	11.5	10.4	8.8
Advanced education	11.9	11.3	10.2	11.4	8.5	10.3
No answer	0.8	0.7	0.8	0.7	0.7	1.1
No male head	27.8	24.7	21.8	26.5	26.5	16.9
Total	100%	100%	100%	100%	100%	100%

*HH = Households

Table 4-8. Profile of Pet-Owning Households, by Education Level of the Female Head of Household, 1991

Education	% All HH*	% Pet HH	% Dog HH	% Cat HH	% Bird HH	% Horse HH
High school or less	39.3	38.9	41.8	37.3	44.5	37.9
Attended college	25.2	28.0	28.4	29.2	29.1	31.8
Graduated college	11.4	12.2	11.2	12.6	9.3	13.0
Advanced education	9.3	9.7	8.8	10.5	6.4	10.0
No answer	0.9	0.8	0.8	0.7	0.9	0.8
No female head	13.8	10.5	9.1	9.8	9.9	6.4
Total	100%	100%	100%	100%	100%	100%

*HH = Households

The life-stage, household income, household size, and home ownership profiles for dog-owning, cat-owning, bird-owning, and horse-owning households are discussed in the following sections.

■ PROFILES OF DOG-OWNING HOUSEHOLDS

Dog-owning households are not likely to be single households (Table 4-9). Specifically, only 13.9% of dog-owning households are young, middle or older singles, whereas 25.9% of all households were single households.

Table 4-9. Profile of Dog-Owning Households, by Life-stage, 1991

Life-stage	All Households (Pct.)	Dog-Owning Households (Pct.)
Young singles	5.2	2.9
Middle singles	10.9	6.7
Older singles	9.8	4.3
Young couple	8.7	9.8
Working older couple	12.0	11.7
Retired older couple	11.4	8.4
Young parents	12.6	14.9
Middle parents	12.9	19.2
Older parents	14.8	20.0
Others	1.8	2.1
Total	100.0	100.0

The majority of dog-owning households are parent households that include one or more children. To illustrate, 54% of dog-owning households are parent households, but only 40% of all households are parent households (Figure 4-3).

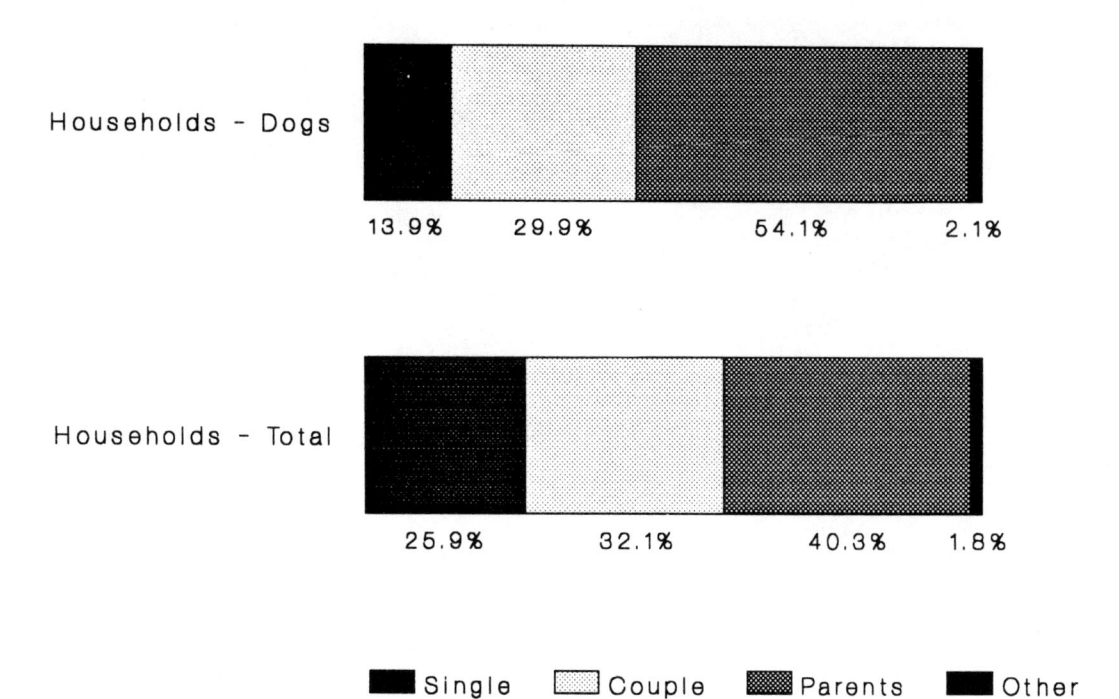

Figure 4-3. Profile of Dog-Owning Households, by Life-stage, 1991

Households - Dogs

| 13.9% | 29.9% | 54.1% | 2.1% |

Households - Total

| 25.9% | 32.1% | 40.3% | 1.8% |

■ Single ☐ Couple ▨ Parents ■ Other

A higher percentage of dog-owning households are in the higher income brackets, compared with all households. Also, a lower percentage of dog-owning households are in the low income brackets. Specifically, 34.3% of dog-owning households have annual incomes under $25,000, but 39.4% of all households have annual incomes under $25,000. Twenty percent of dog-owning households have annual incomes greater than $60,000, but only 18.2% of all households have annual incomes this high (Table 4-10).

Pet Profiles

Table 4-10. Profile of Dog-Owning Households, by Household Income, 1991

Household Income	All Households (Pct.)	Dog-Owning Households (Pct.)
Under $12,500	18.7	14.6
$12,500 to $24,999	20.7	19.7
$25,000 to $39,999	22.4	23.8
$40,000 to $59,999	20.0	21.8
$60,000 and over	18.2	20.0
Total	100.0	100.0

A higher percentage of dog-owning households than of all households are large-member households (Table 4-11). This is consistent with the trend for dog-owning households to be in the parent life-stage demographic group. Fifty-four percent of dog-owning households have 3 or more members; whereas, 42.7% of all households have 3 or more members (Figure 4-4).

Table 4-11. Profile of Dog-Owning Households, by Household Size, 1991

Household Size	All Households (Pct.)	Dog-Owning Households (Pct.)
1 member	24.7	14.0
2 members	32.6	32.5
3 members	17.3	20.5
4 members	15.5	20.4
5 or more members	9.9	12.6
Total	100.0	100.0

Pet Profiles

Figure 4-4. Profile of Dog-Owning Households, by Household Size, 1991

Households - Dogs
14.0% 32.5% 20.5% 33.0%

Households - Total
24.7% 32.6% 17.3% 25.4%

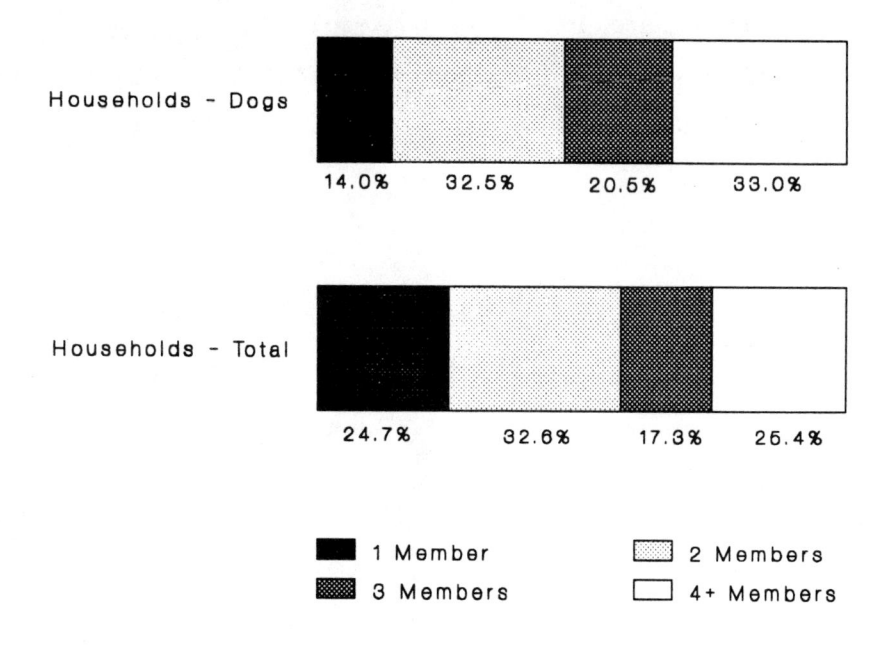

■ 1 Member   ▒ 2 Members
▓ 3 Members   □ 4+ Members

Additionally, dog owners are found to be more likely to own their home and less likely to rent. For dog-owning households, 80.9% own and 13.7% rent their homes (Table 4-12). By comparison, 72.7% of all households own and 21.2% rent their homes.

Table 4-12. Profile of Dog-Owning Households, by Home Ownership, 1991

Home Ownership	All Households (Pct.)	Dog-Owning Households (Pct.)
Own	72.7	80.9
Rent	21.2	13.7
Other*	3.7	3.9
Did not specify	2.5	—
Total	100.0	100.0

*Other = miscellaneous, e.g. living with relatives

AVMA Center for Information Management

Pet Profiles

■ PROFILES OF CAT-OWNING HOUSEHOLDS

Comparisons between cat-owning households and all households reveals that cat owners are more likely to be parent households, and less likely to be single households. Table 4-13 shows that 51% of cat-owning households are young, middle, or older parent households compared with 40% of all households.

Table 4-13. Profile of Cat-Owning Households, by Life-stage, 1991

Life-stage	All Households (Pct.)	Cat-Owning Households (Pct.)
Young singles	5.2	4.5
Middle singles	10.9	8.5
Older singles	9.8	4.6
Young couple	8.7	11.3
Working older couple	12.0	11.0
Retired older couple	11.4	7.3
Young parents	12.6	13.9
Middle parents	12.9	17.8
Older parents	14.8	18.8
Others	1.8	2.3
Total	100.0	100.0

Figure 4-5 illustrates the comparison between single, couple, parent, and other households for cat-owning households and all households.

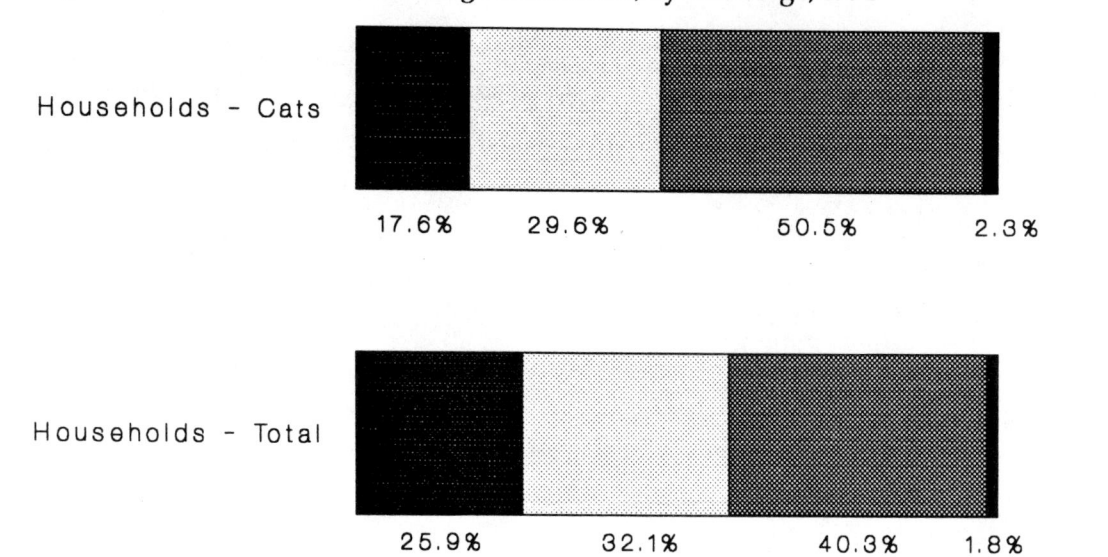

Figure 4-5. Profile of Cat-Owning Households, by Life-stage, 1991

Households - Cats: 17.6% | 29.6% | 50.5% | 2.3%

Households - Total: 25.9% | 32.1% | 40.3% | 1.8%

■ Single ▫ Couple ▨ Parents ■ Other

Slight differences are found between cat-owning households and all households in regard to household income (Table 4-14). Cat-owning households tend to have slightly higher incomes. Sixty-five percent of cat-owning households have annual incomes greater than $25,000, but only 61.6% of all households have annual incomes greater than $25,000.

Table 4-14. Profile of Cat-Owning Households, by Household Income, 1991

Household Income	All Households (Pct.)	Cat-Owning Households (Pct.)
Under $12,500	18.7	14.6
$12,500 to $24,999	20.7	20.4
$25,000 to $39,999	22.4	23.5
$40,000 to $59,999	20.0	21.7
$60,000 and over	18.2	19.8
Total	100.0	100.0

Pet Profiles

Table 4-15. Profile of Cat-Owning Households, by Household Size, 1991

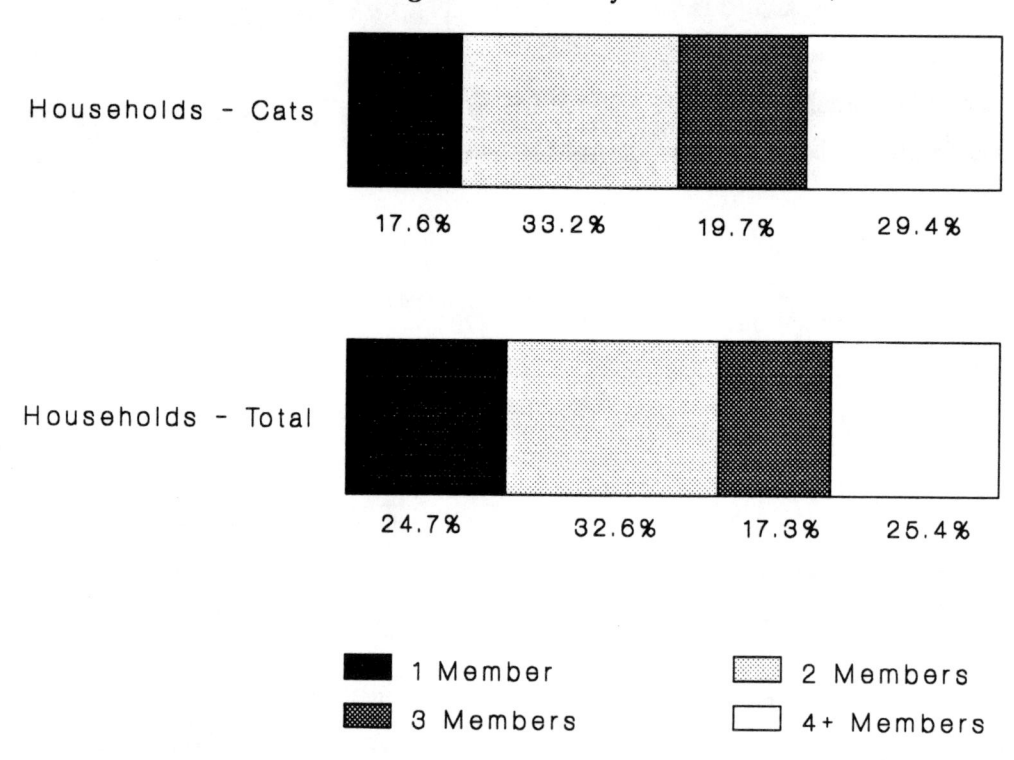

Household Size	All Households (Pct.)	Cat-Owning Households (Pct.)
1 member	24.7	17.6
2 members	32.6	33.2
3 members	17.3	19.7
4 members	15.5	18.1
5 or more members	9.9	11.3
Total	100.0	100.0

Consistent with the trend for cat-owning households to be parent households, cat-owning households tend to be larger households (Table 4-15). Specifically, 49% of cat-owning households are in the 3-or-more-member category, but only 43% of all households are in this category (Figure 4-6).

Figure 4-6. Profile of Cat-Owning Households, by Household Size, 1991

Households - Cats: 17.6% | 33.2% | 19.7% | 29.4%

Households - Total: 24.7% | 32.6% | 17.3% | 25.4%

Legend: 1 Member, 2 Members, 3 Members, 4+ Members

Cat-owning households are more likely than all households to own their home (Table 4-16). Approximately 75% of cat-owning households own their home; whereas, 73% of all households own their home.

Table 4-16. Profile of Cat-Owning Households, by Home Ownership, 1991

Home Ownership	All Households (Pct.)	Cat-Owning Households (Pct.)
Own	72.7	74.8
Rent	21.2	19.5
Other*	3.7	3.9
Did not specify	2.5	—
Total	100.0	100.0

*Other = miscellaneous, e.g. living with relatives

Pet Profiles

■ PROFILES OF BIRD-OWNING HOUSEHOLDS

Bird-owning households are similar to dog-owning and cat-owning households in that bird-owning households are more likely to be parent households, 3-or-more-member households, and households with incomes over $25,000.

Approximately 58.1% of bird-owning households are young, middle, or older parent households, whereas only 40.3% of all households are households in these categories (Table 4-17). Figure 4-7 on the following page illustrates this relationship.

Table 4-17. Profile of Bird-Owning Households, by Life-stage, 1991

Life-stage	All Households (Pct.)	Bird-Owning Households (Pct.)
Young singles	5.2	4.3
Middle singles	10.9	7.5
Older singles	9.8	3.8
Young couple	8.7	9.9
Working older couple	12.0	8.8
Retired older couple	11.4	5.7
Young parents	12.6	14.8
Middle parents	12.9	23.0
Older parents	14.8	20.3
Others	1.8	1.9
Total	100.0	100.0

Figure 4-7. Profile of Bird-Owning Households, by Life-stage, 1991

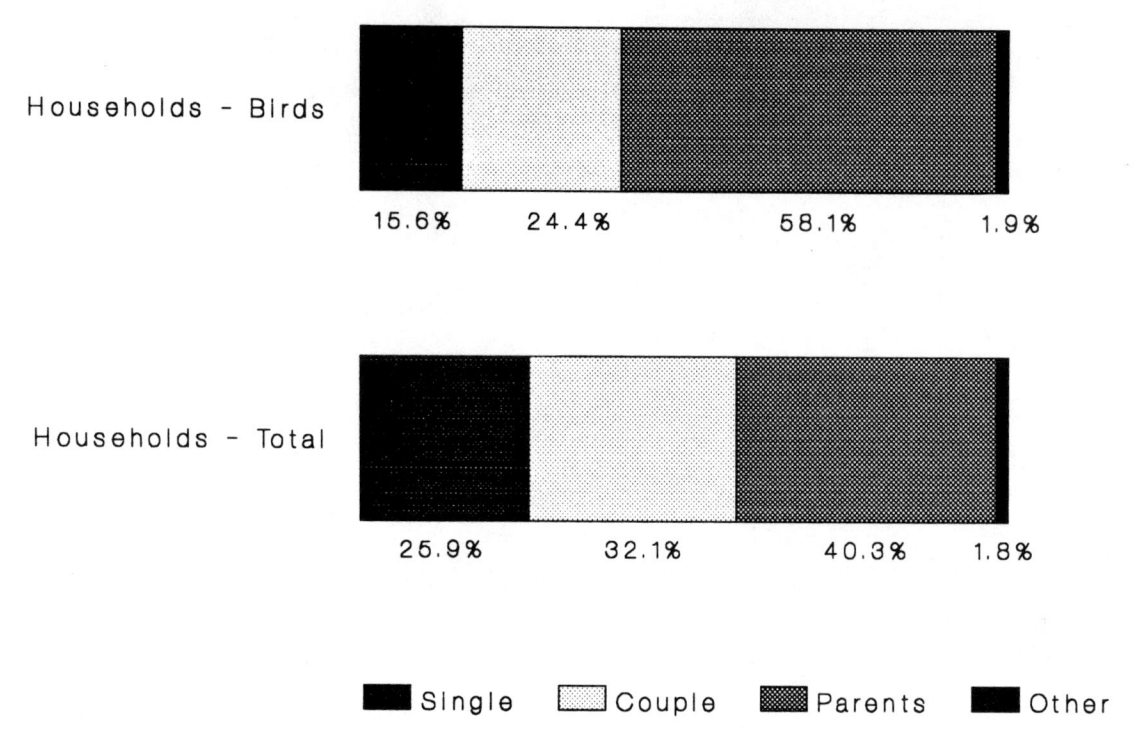

Households - Birds: 15.6% | 24.4% | 58.1% | 1.9%

Households - Total: 25.9% | 32.1% | 40.3% | 1.8%

■ Single □ Couple ▨ Parents ■ Other

Bird-owning households tend to have slightly higher incomes. To summarize across income groups, approximately 63% of bird-owning households have annual incomes over $25,000, and 61% of all households have annual incomes over $25,000 (Table 4-18).

Table 4-18. Profile of Bird-Owning Households, by Household Income, 1991

Household Income	All Households (Pct.)	Bird-Owning Households (Pct.)
Under $12,500	18.7	16.6
$12,500 to $24,999	20.7	20.7
$25,000 to $39,999	22.4	23.9
$40,000 to $59,999	20.0	21.2
$60,000 and over	18.2	17.7
Total	100.0	100.0

Pet Profiles

Table 4-19. Profile of Bird-Owning Households, by Household Size, 1991

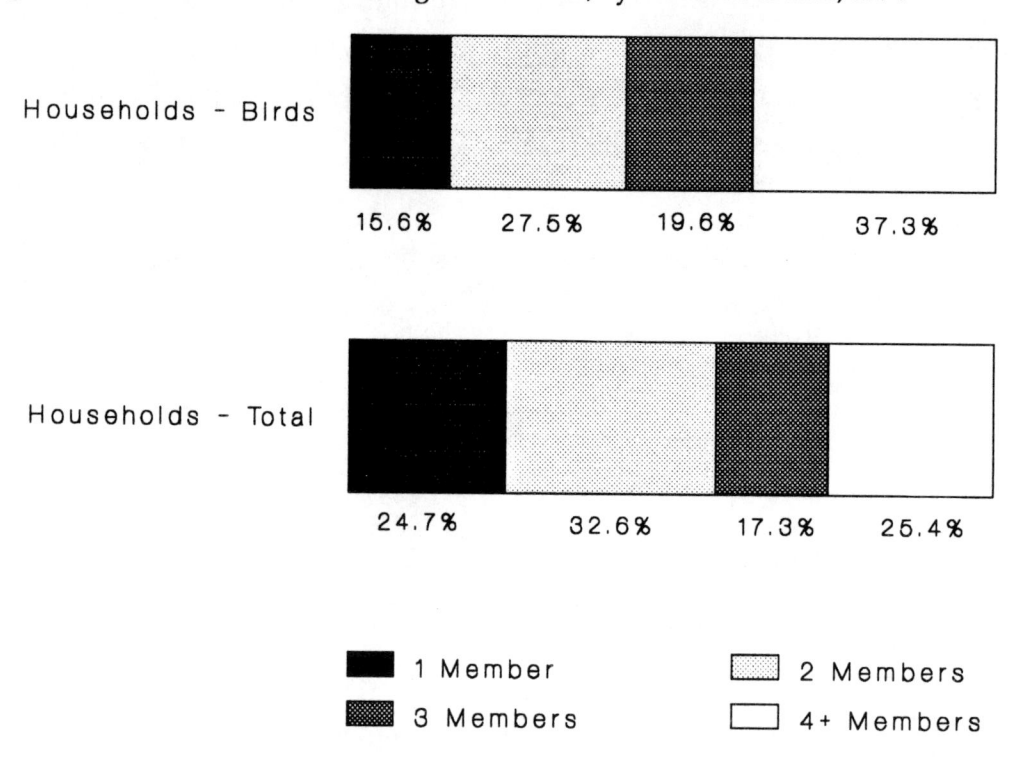

Household Size	All Households (Pct.)	Bird-Owning Households (Pct.)
1 member	24.7	15.6
2 members	32.6	27.5
3 members	17.3	19.6
4 members	15.5	21.4
5 or more members	9.9	15.9
Total	100.0	100.0

Bird-owning households are more likely to be larger households. Specifically, 56.9% of bird-owning households have 3 or more members, but only 42.7% of all households have 3 or more members (Table 4-15). Figure 4-8 illustrates this relationship.

Figure 4-8. Profile of Bird-Owning Households, by Household Size, 1991

Households - Birds: 15.6% 27.5% 19.6% 37.3%

Households - Total: 24.7% 32.6% 17.3% 25.4%

■ 1 Member   ▫ 2 Members
▪ 3 Members   □ 4+ Members

In contrast to dog-owning and cat-owning households, a slightly higher percentage of bird-owning households than of all households, rent their homes. Approximately, 24% of bird-owning households rent and 21% of all households rent (Table 4-20).

Table 4-20. Profile of Bird-Owning Households, by Home Ownership, 1991

Home Ownership	All Households (Pct.)	Bird-Owning Households (Pct.)
Own	72.7	69.4
Rent	21.2	23.9
Other*	3.7	4.5
Did not specify	2.5	—
Total	100.0	100.0

*Other = miscellaneous, e.g. living with relatives

Pet Profiles

■ PROFILES OF HORSE-OWNING HOUSEHOLDS

Grouping horse-owning households by life-stage characteristics reveals that these households are more likely to be couple or parent households than single households or retired, older couple households (Table 4-21).

Of horse-owning households, 54.9% are parent households, whereas of all households, 40.3% are parent households (Figure 4-9). Only 9.4% of horse-owning households are single households, whereas 25.9% of all households are single households.

Table 4-21. Profile of Horse-Owning Households, by Life-stage, 1991

Life-stage	All Households (Pct.)	Horse-Owning Households (Pct.)
Young singles	5.2	3.0
Middle singles	10.9	5.0
Older singles	9.8	1.4
Young couple	8.7	11.2
Working older couple	12.0	14.8
Retired older couple	11.4	8.5
Young parents	12.6	16.1
Middle parents	12.9	18.4
Older parents	14.8	20.4
Others	1.8	1.2
Total	100.0	100.0

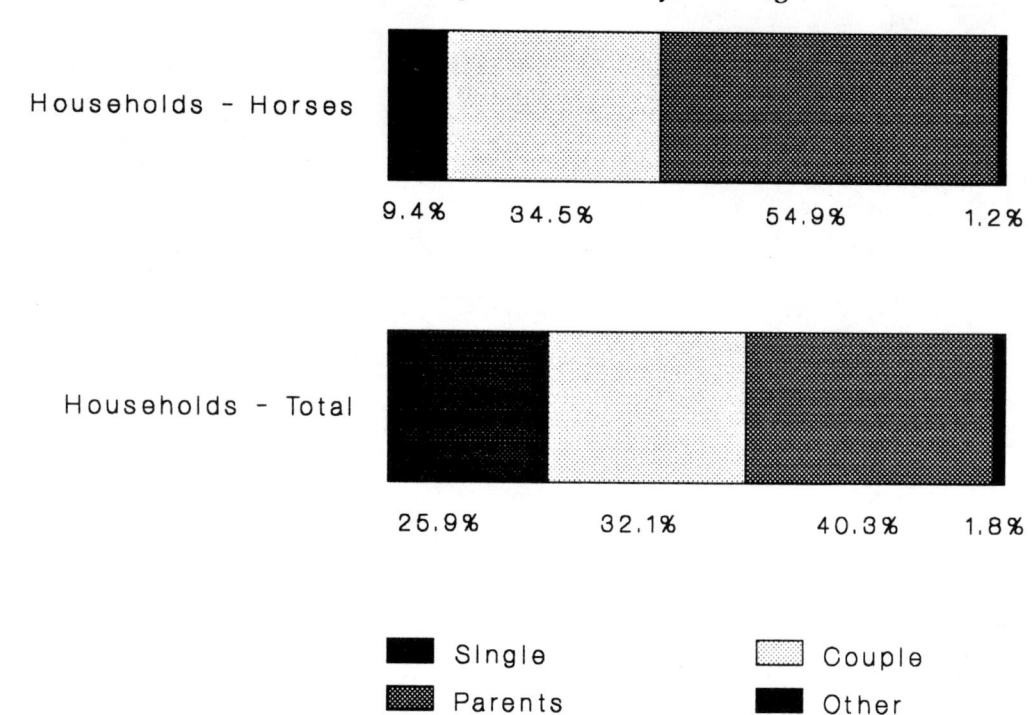

Figure 4-9. Profile of Horse-Owning Households, by Life-stage, 1991

Households - Horses

9.4%   34.5%   54.9%   1.2%

Households - Total

25.9%   32.1%   40.3%   1.8%

- ■ Single
- □ Couple
- ▒ Parents
- ■ Other

Horse owners tend to have somewhat higher household incomes. To summarize, approximately 69% of horse-owning households have annual incomes over $25,000 but only 61% of all households have annual incomes this high (Table 4-22). Less than 40% of horse-owning households have annual incomes of $40,000 or more.

Table 4-22. Profile of Horse-Owning Households, by Household Income, 1991

Household Income	All Households (Pct.)	Horse-Owning Households (Pct.)
Under $12,500	18.7	9.2
$12,500 to $24,999	20.7	21.5
$25,000 to $39,999	22.4	24.8
$40,000 to $59,999	20.0	21.9
$60,000 and over	18.2	22.6
Total	100.0	100.0

Pet Profiles

Table 4-23. Profile of Horse-Owning Households, by Household Size, 1991

Household Size	All Households (Pct.)	Horse-Owning Households (Pct.)
1 member	24.7	9.5
2 members	32.6	34.4
3 members	17.3	20.2
4 members	15.5	21.3
5 or more members	9.9	14.6
Total	100.0	100.0

Horse-owning households also have larger households (Table 4-23). Approximately 9.5% of horse-owning households are 1-member households, and 14.6% are 5-or-more member households. By comparison, 24.7% of all households have 1 member, and 9.9% have 5 or more members (Figure 4-10).

Figure 4-10. Profile of Horse-Owning Households, by Household Size, 1991

Households - Horses: 9.5% | 34.4% | 20.2% | 35.9%

Households - Total: 24.7% | 32.6% | 17.3% | 25.4%

Legend: ■ 1 Member □ 2 Members ▨ 3 Members □ 4+ Members

A higher percentage of horse-owning households than of all households, own their home and a lower percentage rent their home. On average, 82.4% of horse-owning households own their home, and 10.8% rent. By comparison, 72.7% of all households own their home and 21.2% rent.

Table 4-24. Profile of Horse-Owning Households, by Home Ownership, 1991

Home Ownership	All Households (Pct.)	Horse-Owning Households (Pct.)
Own	72.7	82.4
Rent	21.2	10.8
Other*	3.7	5.1
No answer	2.5	—
Total	100.0	100.0

*Other = miscellaneous, e.g. living with relatives

CHAPTER 5

Pet Food and Veterinary Services for Pets

■ PET CARE

In nearly 73% of pet-owning households, a female is the primary animal caretaker (Table 5-1). More specifically, in 38% of pet-owning households, the person most responsible for animal care is a female between 31 and 50 years old. In 20% of pet-owning households, the primary animal caretaker is a female over 50 years old. Figure 5-1 on the next page illustrates the distribution, by gender and age, of persons responsible for pet care in US households.

Table 5-1. Age and Gender of Person Responsible for Pet Care, 1991

Age	Female	Male
Under 30	14.5	6.0
31 to 50	37.9	12.9
Over 50	20.5	8.1
Total	72.9	27.0

Pet Services

Figure 5-1. Age and Gender of Person Responsible for Pet Care, 1991

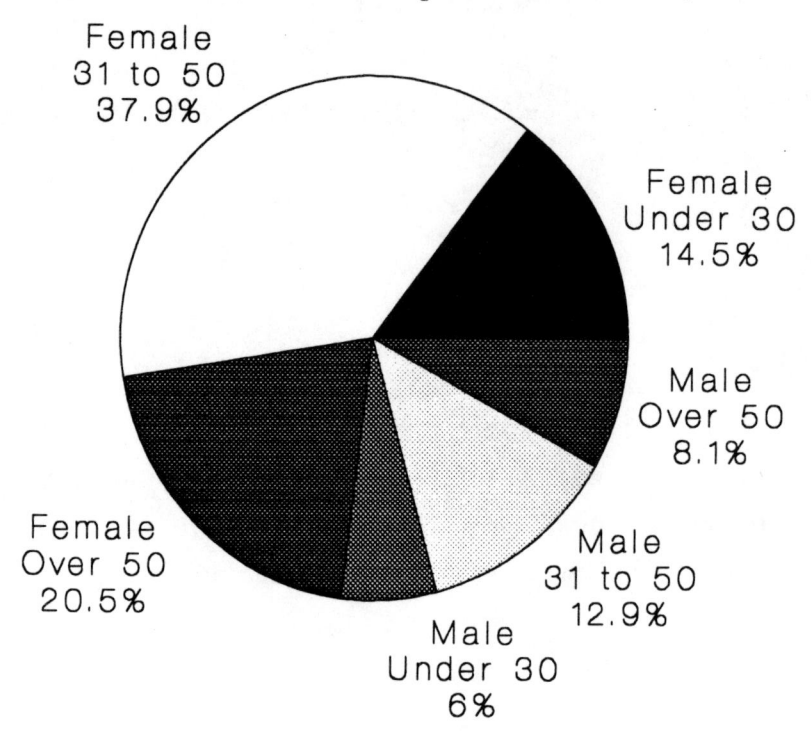

- Female 31 to 50: 37.9%
- Female Under 30: 14.5%
- Male Over 50: 8.1%
- Male 31 to 50: 12.9%
- Male Under 30: 6%
- Female Over 50: 20.5%

■ PET FOOD EXPENDITURES

The mean annual expenditures per pet-owning household for dog, cat, bird, and horse food are listed in Tables 5-2 through 5-5.

Table 5-2.   Expenditures for Dog Food, 1991

Mean expenditures per household	$180.67
Mean expenditures per dog	$115.96

Table 5-3.   Expenditures for Cat Food, 1991

Mean expenditures per household	$143.92
Mean expenditures per cat	$70.88

Table 5-4.   Expenditures for Bird Food, 1991

Mean expenditures per household	$44.13
Mean expenditures per bird	$20.36

Table 5-5.   Expenditures for Horse Food, 1991

Mean expenditures per household	$520.06
Mean expenditures per horse	$204.49

Pet Services

■ DOG VETERINARY SERVICES AND EXPENDITURES

Veterinary care is important for a dog's health, and a large percentage (80%) of dog-owning households have a veterinarian for their dog (Table 5-6).

Table 5-6. Dog-Owning Households That Currently Have a Veterinarian for Their Dogs, 1987, 1991

	1987 (Pct.)	1991 (Pct.)
Have a veterinarian	84.6	79.6
Don't have a veterinarian	15.4	20.4

The decrease in the percentage of households having a veterinarian may be misleading for two reasons. First, the 1987 survey question was slightly different from the 1991 survey question. Second, the 1991 survey results made it possible to determine whether a household had a veterinarian specifically for their dog, even if they owned another pet and had a veterinarian for that other pet. This was not possible with the results of the 1987 survey.

A variety of services and products for dogs are provided during a veterinary visit. Preventive medical services, including vaccinations and physical examinations, are provided more frequently than in 1987. Vaccinations are the most common service provided for 66.6% of dog owners. The percentage of dogs receiving a physical examination during their most recent visit to a veterinarian is 62.0%, an increase from 53.5% in 1987. Approximately 33% of households buy drugs and medications during their last veterinary visit, compared with 42% in 1987. Emergency care is provided approximately 13% of the time, and laboratory testing is performed about 17% of the time.

The findings for dog owners' most recent visit to a veterinarian are listed in Table 5-7.

Table 5-7. Services & Products for Dogs Provided at Most Recent Veterinary Visit, 1987, 1991

Services & Products	1987 (Pct.)	1991 (Pct.)
Physical examination	53.5	62.0
Vaccination	66.0	66.6
Emergency care	13.0	12.6
Neuter/Spay	8.0	8.4
Other surgery	4.9	4.9
Hospitalization	5.0	4.2
X-ray	—	4.1
Lab test	20.5	17.4
Deworming	—	12.6
Flea/Tick products	17.7	13.5
Drugs/Medication	42.4	32.6
Food	10.4	4.4
Vitamins	—	5.3
Dental care	5.5	4.9
Groom/Board	11.4	6.9
Euthanasia	2.8	2.6
Birth/Pregnancy	0.1	—
Eye, nose, throat problems	0.4	—
Skin, hair problems	0.1	—
Other	0.5	2.6
Never examined	1.1	—

Pet Services

Dog owners are relatively heavy consumers of veterinary services, and the trend is continuing upward. Latest figures indicate that 82.3% of dog-owning households have had a dog examined or treated at least once (Table 5-8).

Table 5-8. Veterinary Visits, for Dogs, per Year, 1983, 1987, 1991

Number of Visits	1983 (Pct.)	1987 (Pct.)	1991 (Pct.)
None	26.4	22.4	17.7
One	30.8	23.3	23.2
Two	18.1	22.2	23.1
Three	8.6	11.1	12.3
Four or more	16.1	21.0	23.6
Mean Visits/Household	1.82	2.37	2.64
Mean Visits/Dog	1.09	1.50	1.88

The mean number of veterinary visits per dog-owning household is 2.64 visits, up from 2.37 visits in 1987. The mean number of veterinary visits per dog is 1.88, versus 1.50 in 1987. Figure 5-2 on the next page portrays this trend.

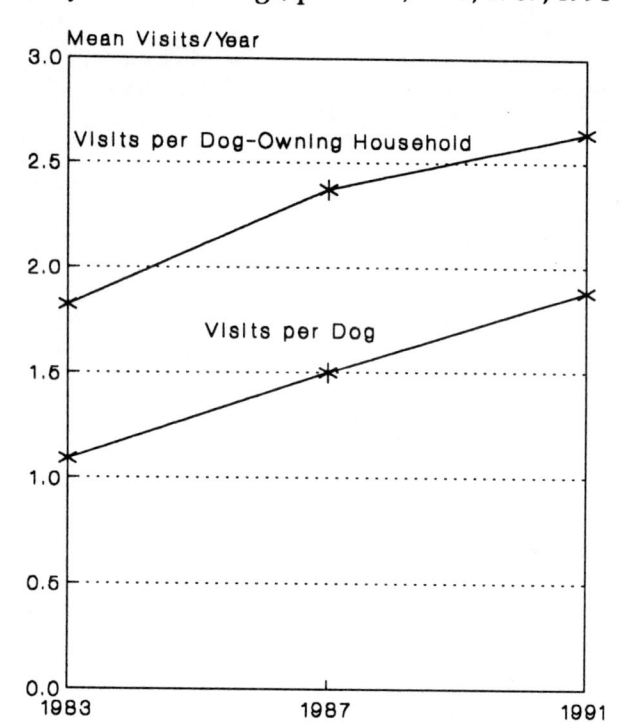

Figure 5-2. Veterinary Visits, for Dogs, per Year, 1983, 1987, 1991

Expenditures for veterinary services have increased since 1987. Mean annual expenditures for veterinary services are estimated to be $131.84 for dog owners, up nearly 60% from $82.68 in 1987 (Table 4-9).

Mean expenditures for veterinary services per visit are $49.96, up 43% from $34.96 in 1987, as illustrated in Figure 5-3 on the next page.

Table 5-9. Veterinary Expenditures, for Dogs, per Year, 1983, 1987, 1991

	1983	1987	1991
Mean expenditures/Household	$66.87	$82.68	$131.84
Mean expenditures/Visit	$37.15	$34.96	$49.96

Pet Services

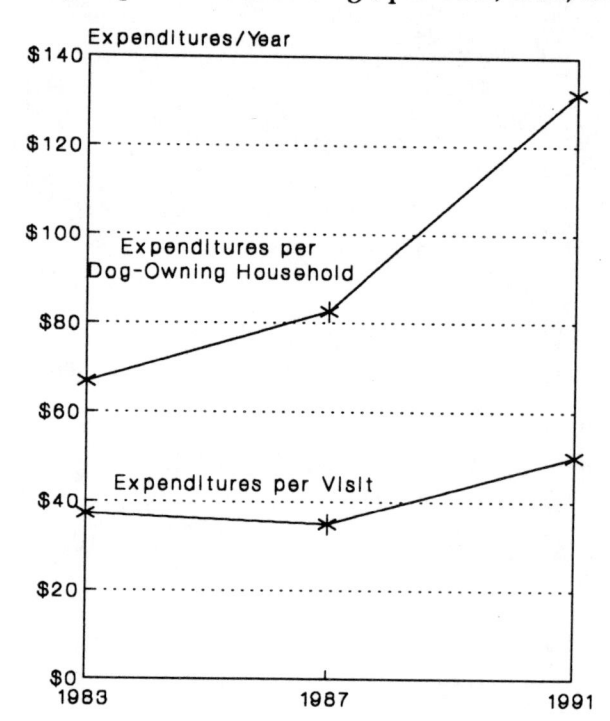

Figure 5-3. Veterinary Expenditures, for Dogs, per Year, 1983, 1987, 1991

Projecting to the national population of dog-owning households, estimated expenditures for veterinary services nationally for dogs are $4.56 billion, up 51% from $3.01 billion in 1987. This increase represents an 11% compounded annual growth rate over the four-year period.

■ CAT VETERINARY SERVICES AND EXPENDITURES

A high percentage of cat owners have a veterinarian, even though the percentage is a decrease from four years earlier. Seventy percent of cat-owning households have a veterinarian (Table 5-10). The decrease in the percentage of cat owners having a veterinarian may be a result of differences between the 1987 and 1991 surveys' question and the method for tabulation of results.

Table 5-10. Cat-Owning Households That Currently Have a Veterinarian for Their Cats, 1987, 1991

	1987 (Pct.)	1991 (Pct.)
Have a veterinarian	78.4	70.2
Don't have a veterinarian	21.6	29.8

Cat owners and veterinarians are developing responsible health care programs for cats. During their most recent visit to a veterinarian, cats were provided a variety of services and products, mainly preventive services (Table 5-11). The percentage of cats receiving a vaccination is 64.4%, an increase from 60.9% in 1987. Physical examinations are performed 49.8% of the time in 1987, but 58.6% of the time in 1991. Drugs and medications are provided for 22.8% of households, 19.6% of cats are spayed or castrated during their most recent visit to a veterinarian.

Pet Services

Table 5-11. Services & Products for Cats Provided at Most Recent Veterinary Visit, 1987, 1991

Services & Products	1987 (Pct.)	1991 (Pct.)
Physical examination	49.8	58.6
Vaccination	60.9	64.4
Emergency care	15.3	13.6
Neuter/Spay	21.4	19.6
Other surgery	7.4	6.2
Hospitalization	6.7	5.5
X-ray	—	3.2
Lab test	14.7	12.5
Deworming	—	10.4
Flea/Tick products	11.6	9.5
Drugs/Medication	32.5	22.8
Food	8.3	6.7
Vitamins	—	2.7
Dental care	4.7	4.9
Groom/Board	4.6	3.5
Euthanasia	3.0	2.6
Birth/Pregnancy	0.0	—
Eye, nose, throat problems	0.2	—
Skin, hair problems	0.0	—
Other	0.4	3.5
Never examined	2.8	—

A trend towards increasing numbers of veterinary visits has been evident since 1983. During 1991, approximately 62% of cat-owning households visit the veterinarian at least once. Specifically, 23.1% have seen the veterinarian one time; 17.5%, two times; 7.6%, three times; and 14.2%, four-or-more times (Table 5-12).

Table 5-12. Veterinary Visits, for Cats, per Year, 1983, 1987, 1991

Number of Visits	1983 (Pct.)	1987 (Pct.)	1991 (Pct.)
None	52.8	40.6	37.6
One	23.8	22.5	23.1
Two	11.4	16.2	17.5
Three	4.8	7.5	7.6
Four or more	7.2	13.3	14.2
Mean Visits/Household	0.95	1.62	1.78
Mean Visits/Cat	0.40	0.79	0.88

On average, cat owners visit the veterinarian 1.78 times per household compared with 1.62 times per household during 1987 (Figure 5-4).

Figure 5-4. Veterinary Visits, for Cats, per Year, 1983, 1987, 1991

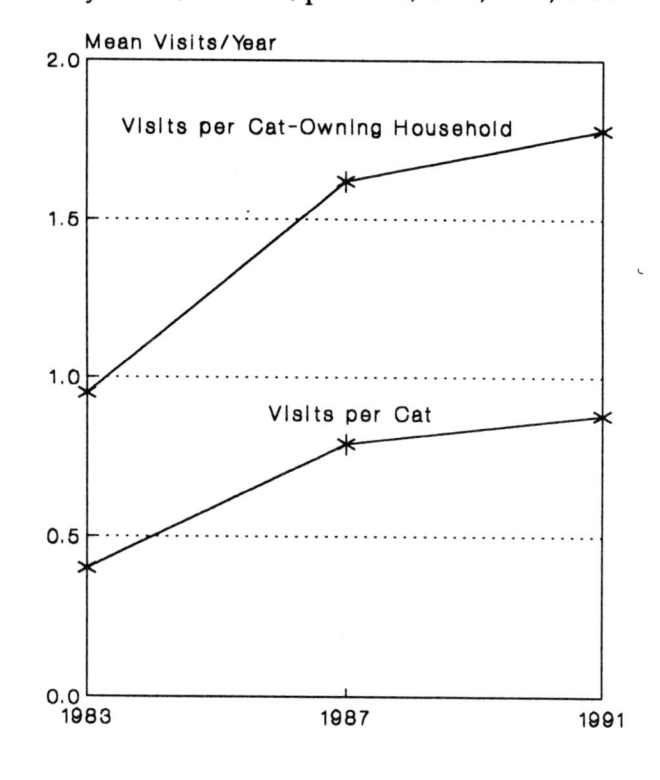

Pet Services

Table 5-13. Veterinary Expenditures, for Cats, per Year, 1983, 1987, 1991

	1983	1987	1991
Mean expenditures/Household	$36.83	$54.26	$79.75
Mean expenditures/Visit	$38.77	$33.59	$44.81

Expenditures for veterinary visits have increased during the four years between surveys. Cat-owning households spend $79.75, on average, per year, compared with $54.26 in 1987 (Table 5-13). Mean expenditures per visit are $44.81, compared with $33.59 in 1987 (Figure 5-5).

Figure 5-5. Veterinary Expenditures, for Cats, per Year, 1983, 1987, 1991

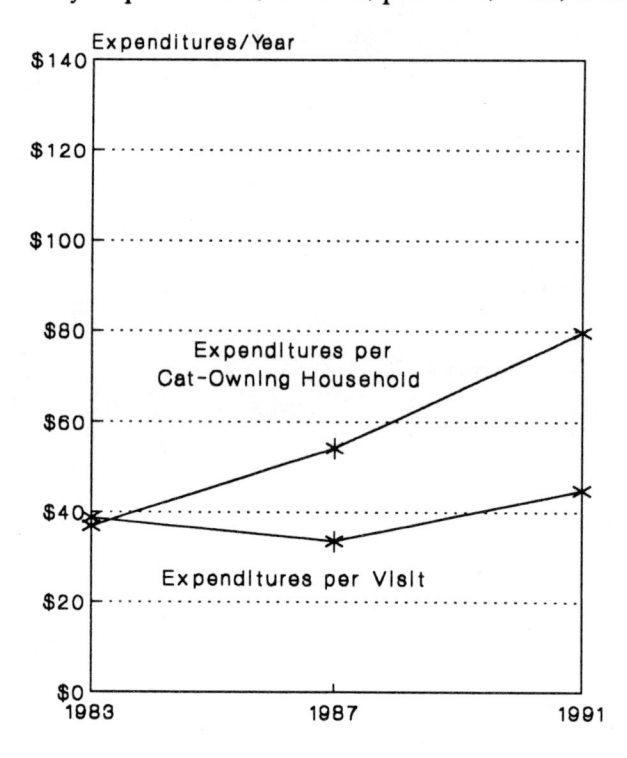

Projecting to the national population of cat-owning households, estimated expenditures nationally for veterinary services for cats are $2.33 billion, up 48% from $1.57 billion in 1987.

■ BIRD VETERINARY SERVICES AND EXPENDITURES

Use of veterinary services is low among bird owners, unlike dog and cat owners. The percentage of households who indicate that they currently have a veterinarian for their pet bird is 21%, down from 30.3% in 1987 (Table 5-14). This decrease may be a result of changes in the survey question and tabulation method between 1987 and 1991.

Table 5-14. Bird-Owning Households That Currently Have a Veterinarian for Their Birds, 1987, 1991

	1987 (Pct.)	1991 (Pct.)
Have a veterinarian	30.3	21.0
Don't have a veterinarian	69.7	79.0

Consistent with the small percentage of bird owners that have a veterinarian, there is a small percentage of pet birds receiving preventive medical services. Physical examinations are provided for 40.4% of the bird owners during their most recent visit to a veterinarian, an increase from 32.4% in 1987. Emergency care is provided for nearly 23% of bird owners. Another 34.2% of bird owners visit the veterinarian for other unspecified reasons (Table 5-15).

Table 5-15. Services & Products for Birds Provided at Most Recent Veterinary Visit, 1987, 1991

Services & Products	1987 (Pct.)	1991 (Pct.)
Physical examination	32.4	40.4
Vaccination	17.6	5.5
Emergency care	14.7	22.7
Neuter/Spay	1.0	0.2
Other surgery	1.0	1.6
Hospitalization	3.9	3.1
X-ray	—	1.8
Lab test	10.8	10.8
Deworming	—	0.7
Flea/Tick products	4.9	1.8
Drugs/Medication	24.5	15.4
Food	10.8	4.4
Vitamins	—	6.6
Dental care	2.0	0.7
Groom/Board	11.8	7.3
Euthanasia	5.9	1.6
Other	1.0	34.2
Never examined	28.4	—

The number of veterinary visits for pet birds is low. The mean number of veterinary visits per bird-owning household is 0.22. Nearly 90% of bird owners do not have their bird seen by a veterinarian. Six percent of bird owners make one visit to the veterinarian and 4% make two or more visits (Table 5-16).

Table 5-16. Veterinary Visits, for Birds, per Year, 1991

Number of Visits	1991 (Pct.)
None	89.4
One	6.3
Two	2.4
Three	0.5
Four or more	1.2
Mean Visits/Household	0.22
Mean Visits/Bird	0.10

Bird-owning households spend an average of $7.60 per household per year for veterinary services, compared with $4.47 in 1987. Mean annual expenditures per visit for bird owners are $34.24 per year (Table 5-17).

Projecting these figures to the national level, total estimated expenditures for bird veterinary services are $185 million.

Table 5-17. Veterinary Expenditures, for Birds, per Year, 1987, 1991

	1987	1991
Mean expenditures/Household	$4.47	$7.60
Mean expenditures/Visit	$29.68	$34.24

Pet Services

■ HORSE VETERINARY SERVICES AND EXPENDITURES

The percentage of horse owners who indicated that they currently have a veterinarian is 67.9%. This is lower than the 1987 estimate of 73.6% (Table 5-18). Again, the changes in tabulation method and survey questions between 1987 and 1991 may be a reason for the decreased use of veterinarians.

Table 5-18. Horse-Owning Households That Currently Have a Veterinarian for Their Horses, 1987, 1991

	1987 (Pct.)	1991 (Pct.)
Have a veterinarian	73.6	67.9
Don't have a veterinarian	26.4	32.1

Table 5-19. Services & Products for Horses Provided at Most Recent Veterinary Visit, 1987, 1991

Services & Products	1987 (Pct.)	1991 (Pct.)
Physical examination	30.2	38.1
Vaccination	52.8	42.6
Emergency care	20.8	27.4
Neuter/Spay	3.8	3.3
Other surgery	3.8	4.5
Hospitalization	1.9	0.8
X-ray	—	2.3
Lab test	18.9	9.1
Deworming	—	27.9
Flea/Tick products	3.8	0.7
Drugs/Medication	52.8	24.7
Food	9.4	0.7
Vitamins	—	2.7
Dental care	11.3	9.1
Groom/Board	7.5	1.0
Euthanasia	3.8	1.5
Other	1.9	7.4

Although a large percentage of horse owners have a veterinarian, a small percentage of horses receive preventive medical services during their most recent visit to a veterinarian. Approximately 38% of horses receive a physical examination, compared with 30% in 1987. Although 52.8% received vaccinations in 1987, only 42.6% did in 1991. The frequency with which drugs and medications are provided by veterinarians decreased from 52.8% in 1987 to 24.7% in 1991. Emergency care services have increased in frequency to 27.4% from 20.8% in 1987, and 27.9% of horse owners obtained deworming services for their horses (Table 5-19).

Table 5-20. Veterinary Visits, for Horses, per Year, 1991

Number of Visits	1991 (Pct.)
None	46.4
One	17.2
Two	14.4
Three	6.5
Four or more	15.4
Mean Visits/Household	2.40
Mean Visits/Horse	0.94

Horse owners visit their veterinarian, on average, 2.4 times per household per year (Table 5-20). Approximately 54% of the horse-owning households visit the veterinarian at least once. More specifically, 17.2% visit the veterinarian one time; 14.4%, two times; 6.5%, three times; and 15.4%, four-or-more times.

The mean number of visits per horse per year is 0.94 times, or nearly one visit per year.

Pet Services

Horse-owning households spend, on average, $163 per household on veterinary services (Table 5-21). This compares with an estimated $121, on average, in 1987. Mean annual expenditures per visit for horse owners are $68.

Table 5-21. Veterinary Expenditures, for Horses, per Year, 1987, 1991

	1987	1991
Mean expenditures/Household	$120.75	$163.23
Mean expenditures/Visit	$65.27	$68.10

Projecting these figures to a national level, total estimated expenditures for household-owned horse veterinary services are $314 million.

This veterinary expenditure estimate does not represent all expenditures for horses, because commercial and other horse establishments are not included in the survey.

■ OTHER PET VETERINARY SERVICES AND EXPENDITURES

The percentage of households that have seen a veterinarian for their other pets varies significantly. Although fish have the highest population, less than one percent of fish owners visit a veterinarian for their fish. Nearly 16% of rabbit owners, 13% of guinea pig owners, and 56% of ferret owners have visited a veterinarian (Table 5-22).

Table 5-22. Other Pet-Owning Households That Obtain Veterinary Care, 1991

Other Pets	Percentage
Fish	0.29
Rabbit	15.96
Hamster	5.02
Guinea Pig	12.70
Gerbil	1.99
Ferret	56.25
Other Rodents	11.63
Turtle	6.85
Snake	13.33
Lizard	6.5
Other Reptiles	2.94
Other Birds	3.85
Livestock	30.17
All Others	5.88

Pet Services

The mean number of veterinary visits per household per year for other pet species is 0.23. This is equivalent to a pet owner taking their pet to the veterinarian once every four years.

Mean expenditures per household for veterinary services are $9.05, compared with $7.74 in 1987. On a per visit basis (which occurred only once every four years), expenditures are $40.12, compared with $27.64 in 1987 (Table 5-23).

Table 5-23. Veterinary Visits and Expenditures for Other Pets, 1987, 1991

Other Pets	1987	1991
Mean Visits/Household	0.28	0.23
Expenditures/Household	$7.74	$9.05
Expenditures/Visit	$27.64	$40.12

CHAPTER 6

Veterinary Medical Profession

■ VETERINARY MEDICINE

The veterinary medical profession is dedicated to protecting the health and welfare of all animals. Veterinarians are highly educated and skilled in preventing, diagnosing, and treating animal health problems. Veterinarians also protect people by preventing and controlling diseases transmissible from animals to human beings.

■ AMERICAN VETERINARY MEDICAL ASSOCIATION

The American Veterinary Medical Association (AVMA) is the professional organization for veterinarians. The AVMA acts on behalf of the veterinary profession to present its views to government, academia, agriculture, animal owners, the media, and other concerned parties. Through the AVMA Foundation, the AVMA supports research to improve animal and human health.

■ NATION

The population of active veterinarians in the US increased 48.7% from 32,734 in 1980 to 48,666 in 1990, or about 4% per year, compounded annually. The current total number of active veterinarians is estimated to be 50,173 (Figure 6-1). Generally, the veterinary medical profession is growing approximately 3% per year.

Veterinary Medical Profession

Figure 6-1. Veterinarians, 1980, 1990, 1991

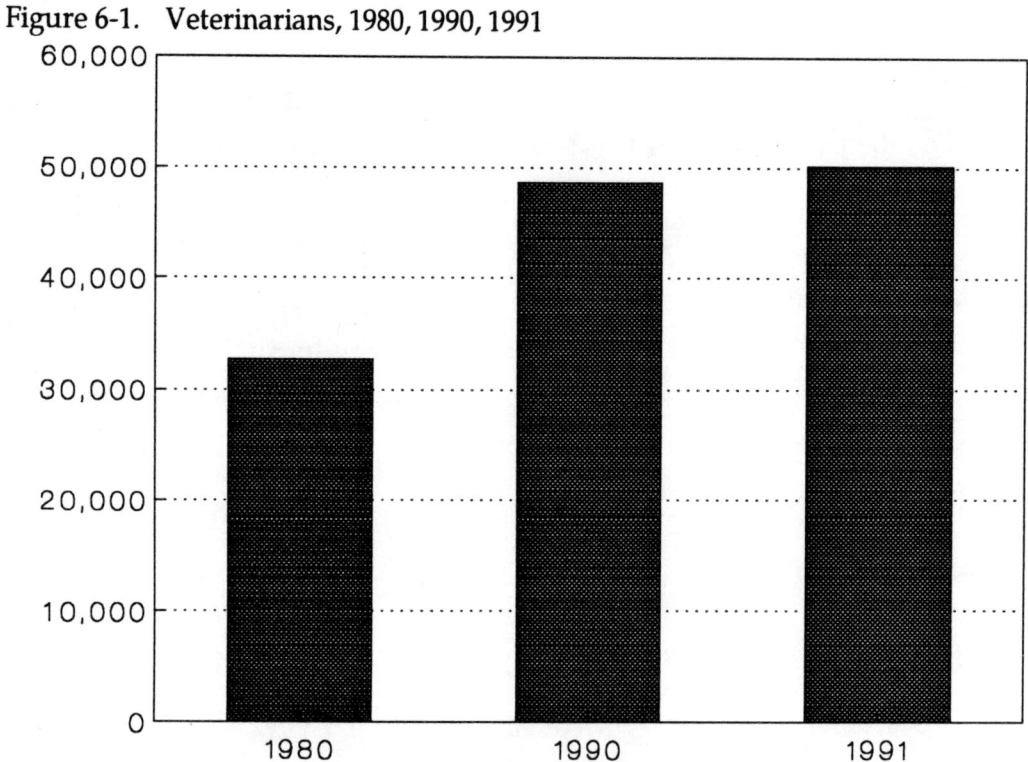

Figure 6-2. Percentage Change in the Number of Veterinarians, by State, 1980 - 1990

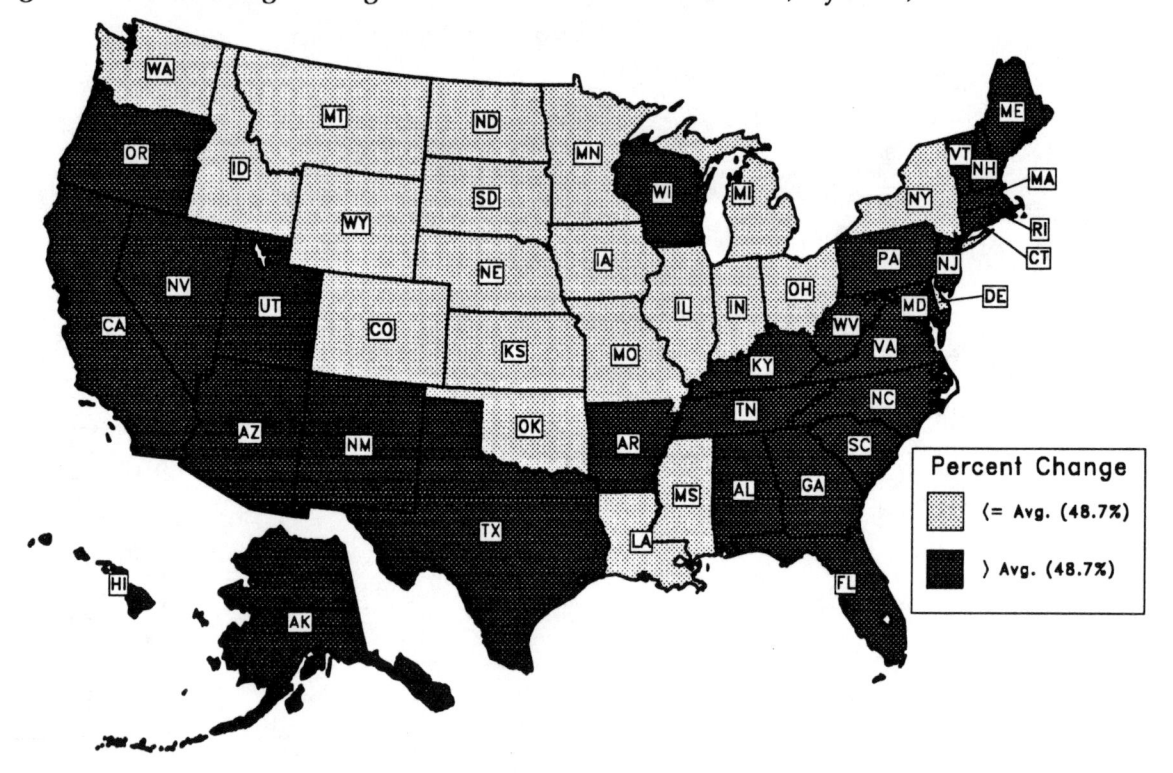

■ STATE

The percentage increase in veterinarians from 1980 to 1990 varied among states. Nevada had the highest growth rate (108.3%) from 1980 to 1990. Growth in Iowa and North Dakota increased by 8.0% or less over the ten-year period. In general, greater-than-average growth occurred in coastal states, and less-than-average growth occurred in north central and western mountain states (Figure 6-2).

Analysis by geographic region shows that the West North Central region had the lowest growth rate (27.4%) from 1980 to 1990. The South Atlantic and New England regions had growth rates over the ten-year period of 76.4% and 74%, respectively. As a result, the South Atlantic replaces the East North Central as the region with the most veterinarians.

California has the largest population of veterinarians, with approximately 10% of all veterinarians in the nation. More than 26% of US veterinarians are located in California, Texas, Florida, and New York combined (Table 6-1).

Table 6-1. Veterinarians, by State, 1980, 1990, 1991

State	1980 No.	1980 Pct.	1990 No.	1990 Pct.	1991 No.	1991 Pct.	Change 1980-1990 No.	Change 1980-1990 Pct.
Total	32,734	100.0	48,666	100.0	50,173	100.0	15,932	48.7
New England	1,333	4.1	2,319	4.8	2,398	4.8	986	74.0
Maine	146	0.4	240	0.5	247	0.5	94	64.4
New Hampshire	141	0.4	256	0.5	264	0.5	115	81.6
Vermont	119	0.4	198	0.4	208	0.4	79	66.4
Massachusetts	512	1.6	942	1.9	973	1.9	430	84.0
Rhode Island	59	0.2	110	0.2	107	0.2	51	86.4
Connecticut	356	1.1	573	1.2	599	1.2	217	61.0
Middle Atlantic	3,551	10.8	5,382	11.1	5,542	11.0	1,831	51.6
New York	1,582	4.8	2,336	4.8	2,396	4.8	754	47.7
New Jersey	744	2.3	1,159	2.4	1,174	2.3	415	55.8
Pennsylvania	1,225	3.7	1,887	3.9	1,972	3.9	662	54.0
East North Central	5,982	18.3	8,077	16.6	8,278	16.5	2,095	35.0
Ohio	1,397	4.3	1,876	3.9	1,905	3.8	479	34.3
Indiana	922	2.8	1,148	2.4	1,160	2.3	226	24.5
Illinois	1,482	4.5	1,964	4.0	2,023	4.0	482	32.5
Michigan	1,293	4.0	1,663	3.4	1,704	3.4	370	28.6
Wisconsin	888	2.7	1,426	2.9	1,486	3.0	538	60.6

Veterinary Medical Profession

Table 6-1. Veterinarians, by State, 1980, 1990, 1991 (continued)

State	1980 No.	1980 Pct.	1990 No.	1990 Pct.	1991 No.	1991 Pct.	Change 1980-1990 No.	Change 1980-1990 Pct.
West North Central	4,345	13.3	5,535	11.4	5,719	11.4	1,190	27.4
Minnesota	871	2.7	1,231	2.5	1,274	2.5	360	41.3
Iowa	1,121	3.4	1,203	2.5	1,238	2.5	82	7.3
Missouri	907	2.8	1,197	2.5	1,234	2.5	290	32.0
North Dakota	125	0.4	135	0.3	144	0.3	10	8.0
South Dakota	204	0.6	248	0.5	251	0.5	44	21.6
Nebraska	448	1.4	586	1.2	613	1.2	138	30.8
Kansas	669	2.0	935	1.9	965	1.9	266	39.8
South Atlantic	4,784	14.6	8,439	17.3	8,751	17.4	3,655	76.4
Delaware	80	0.2	109	0.2	128	0.3	29	36.3
Maryland	763	2.3	1,242	2.6	1,276	2.5	479	62.8
Virginia	719	2.2	1,353	2.8	1,408	2.8	634	88.2
Dist. of Columbia	72	0.2	79	0.2	74	0.1	7	9.7
West Virginia	133	0.4	201	0.4	198	0.4	68	51.1
North Carolina	649	2.0	1,352	2.8	1,417	2.8	703	108.3
South Carolina	255	0.8	442	0.9	463	0.9	187	73.3
Georgia	749	2.3	1,227	2.5	1,279	2.5	478	63.8
Florida	1,364	4.2	2,434	5.0	2,508	5.0	1,070	78.4
East South Central	1,905	5.8	2,936	6.0	3,012	6.0	1,031	54.1
Kentucky	501	1.5	776	1.6	794	1.6	275	54.9
Tennessee	561	1.7	904	1.9	917	1.8	343	61.1
Alabama	538	1.6	837	1.7	874	1.7	299	55.6
Mississippi	305	0.9	419	0.9	427	0.9	114	37.4
West South Central	3,745	11.4	5,523	11.3	5,665	11.3	1,778	47.5
Arkansas	304	0.9	455	0.9	460	0.9	151	49.7
Louisiana	516	1.6	745	1.5	762	1.5	229	44.4
Oklahoma	623	1.9	892	1.8	895	1.8	269	43.2
Texas	2,302	7.0	3,431	7.1	3,548	7.1	1,129	49.0
Mountain	2,389	7.3	3,487	7.2	3,592	7.2	1,098	46.0
Montana	241	0.7	295	0.6	292	0.6	54	22.4
Idaho	259	0.8	325	0.7	329	0.7	66	25.5
Wyoming	128	0.4	158	0.3	166	0.3	30	23.4
Colorado	840	2.6	1,144	2.4	1,196	2.4	304	36.2
New Mexico	203	0.6	354	0.7	362	0.7	151	74.4
Arizona	424	1.3	706	1.5	731	1.5	282	66.5
Utah	158	0.5	241	0.5	253	0.5	83	52.5
Nevada	136	0.4	264	0.5	263	0.5	128	94.1
Pacific	4,524	13.8	6,737	13.8	6,977	13.9	2,213	48.9
Washington	826	2.5	1,163	2.4	1,230	2.5	337	40.8
Oregon	472	1.4	707	1.5	739	1.5	235	49.8
California	3,048	9.3	4,588	9.4	4,710	9.4	1,540	50.5
Alaska	77	0.2	124	0.3	133	0.3	47	61.0
Hawaii	101	0.3	155	0.3	165	0.3	54	53.5
Possessions	176	0.5	231	0.5	239	0.5	55	31.3
Puerto Rico	57	0.2	104	0.2	109	0.2	47	82.5
Other Possessions	119	0.4	127	0.3	130	0.3	8	6.7

Veterinary Medical Profession

Figures 6-3 and 6-4 illustrate the geographic distribution of veterinarians in 1980 and 1990 and in 1991, respectively.

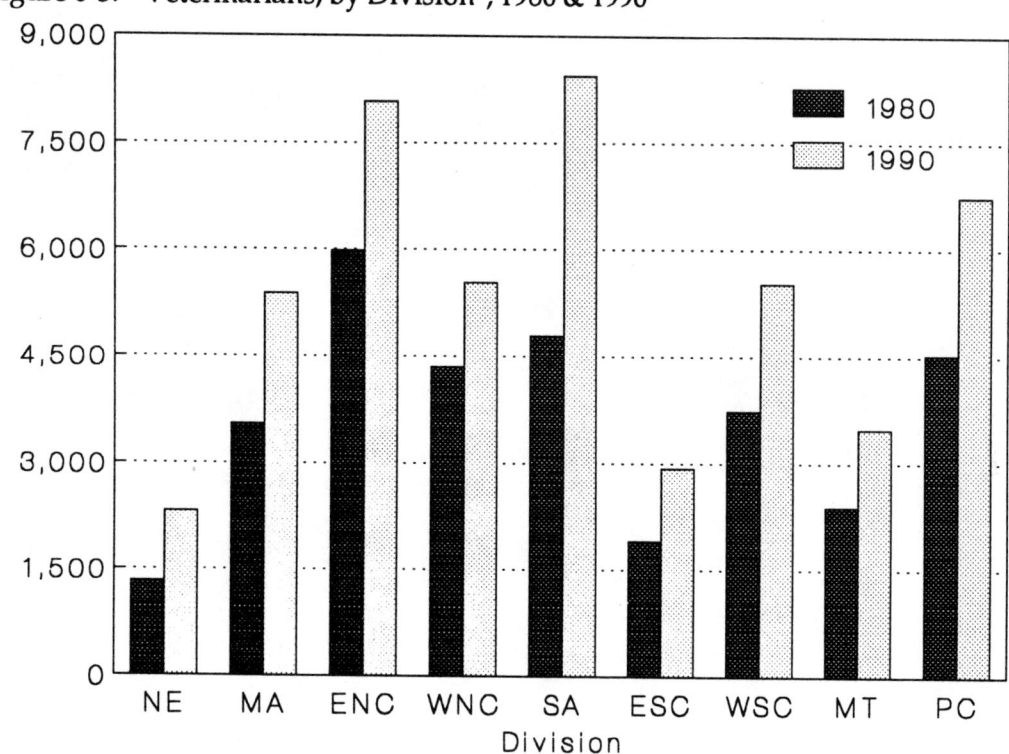

Figure 6-3. Veterinarians, by Division*, 1980 & 1990

*Division: NE = New England; MA = Middle Atlantic; ENC = East North Central; WNC = West North Central; SA = South Atlantic; ESC = East South Central; WSC = West South Central; MT = Mountain; PC = Pacific

Veterinary Medical Profession

Figure 6-4. Veterinarians, by Division*, 1991

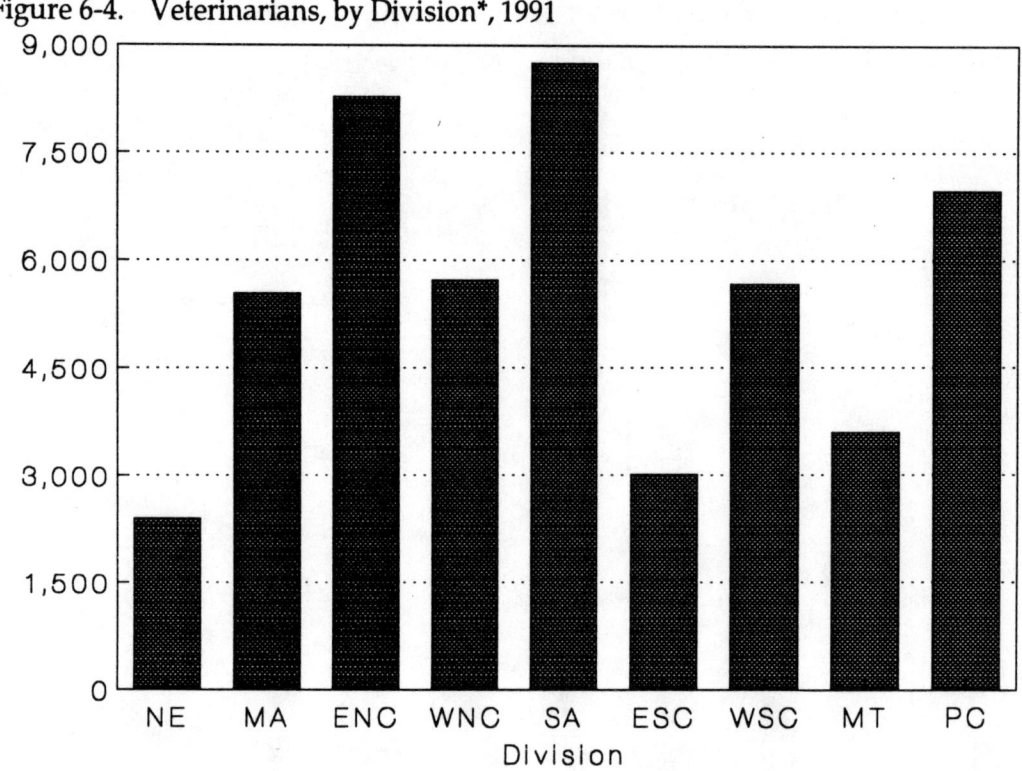

*Division: NE = New England; MA = Middle Atlantic; ENC = East North Central; WNC = West North Central; SA = South Atlantic; ESC = East South Central; WSC = West South Central; MT = Mountain; PC = Pacific

Veterinary Medical Profession

■ GENDER

The composition of the veterinary medical profession changed from 1980 to 1990 as more females than males entered veterinary medicine. The number of female veterinarians increased 288% during the ten-year period, whereas, the number of male veterinarians increased only 24%.

In 1980, approximately 90% of veterinarians were male and 10% were female (Table 6-2). Currently, 27% of veterinarians are female, and 73% are male. In just over ten years, the proportion of females increased from one of ten veterinarians to one of four veterinarians (Figure 6-5).

Table 6-2. Veterinarians, by Gender, 1980, 1990, 1991

Gender	1980 No.	1980 Pct.	1990 No.	1990 Pct.	1991 No.	1991 Pct.	Change 1980-1990 No.	Change 1980-1990 Pct.
Total	32,500	100.0	48,666	100.0	50,173	100.0	16,166	49.7
Female	3,212	9.9	12,462	25.6	13,555	27.0	9,250	288.0
Male	29,288	90.1	36,204	74.4	36,618	73.0	6,916	23.6

Figure 6-5. Veterinarians, by Gender, 1980, 1990, 1991

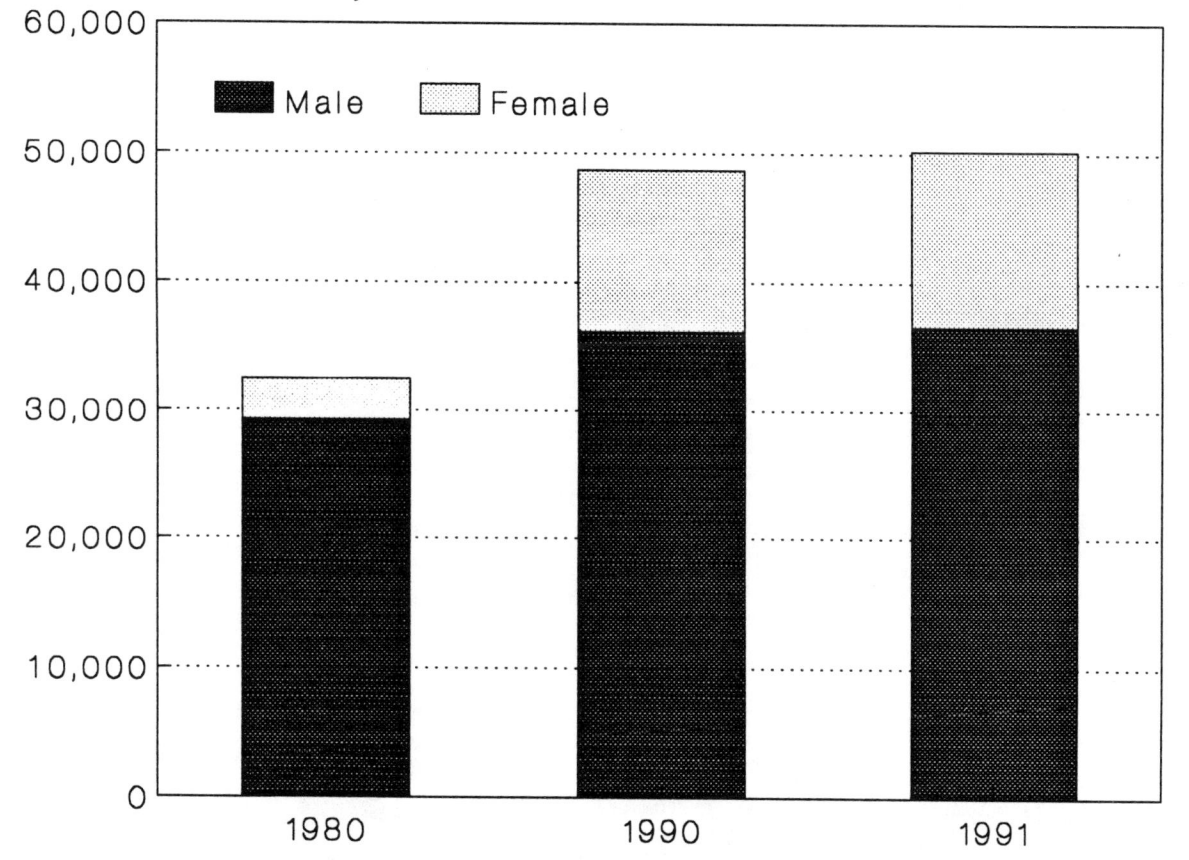

Veterinary Medical Profession

■ AGE

The median age of the veterinary profession is 39 years, unchanged from 1980. This indicates that one-half of the veterinary profession is younger than 39 years of age and one-half is older. With the exception of the "under 30" age group, the number of veterinarians in each age group increased from 1980 to 1990 (Table 6-3).

Figures 6-6 and 6-7 illustrate the distribution of veterinarians by age groups in 1980 and 1990 and in 1991, respectively.

Table 6-3. Veterinarians, by Age, 1980, 1990, 1991

Age (years)	1980 No.	1980 Pct.	1990 No.	1990 Pct.	1991 No.	1991 Pct.	Change 1980-1990 No.	Change 1980-1990 Pct.
Total	32,482	100.0	48,525	100.0	50,035	100.0	16,043	49.4
Under 30	5,764	17.7	5,444	11.2	5,327	10.6	-320	-5.6
30 to 34	6,906	21.3	9,613	19.8	9,501	19.0	2,707	39.2
35 to 39	5,231	16.1	10,050	20.7	10,375	20.7	4,819	92.1
40 to 44	3,179	9.8	7,691	15.8	8,143	16.3	4,512	141.9
45 to 49	3,237	10.0	5,183	10.7	5,736	11.5	1,946	60.1
50 to 54	2,545	7.8	3,112	6.4	3,300	6.6	567	22.3
55 to 59	2,757	8.5	2,973	6.1	2,997	6.0	216	7.8
60 and over	2,863	8.8	4,459	9.2	4,656	9.3	1,596	55.7
Median Age	38	—	39	—	39	—	—	—

Figure 6-6. Veterinarians, by Age, 1980 & 1990

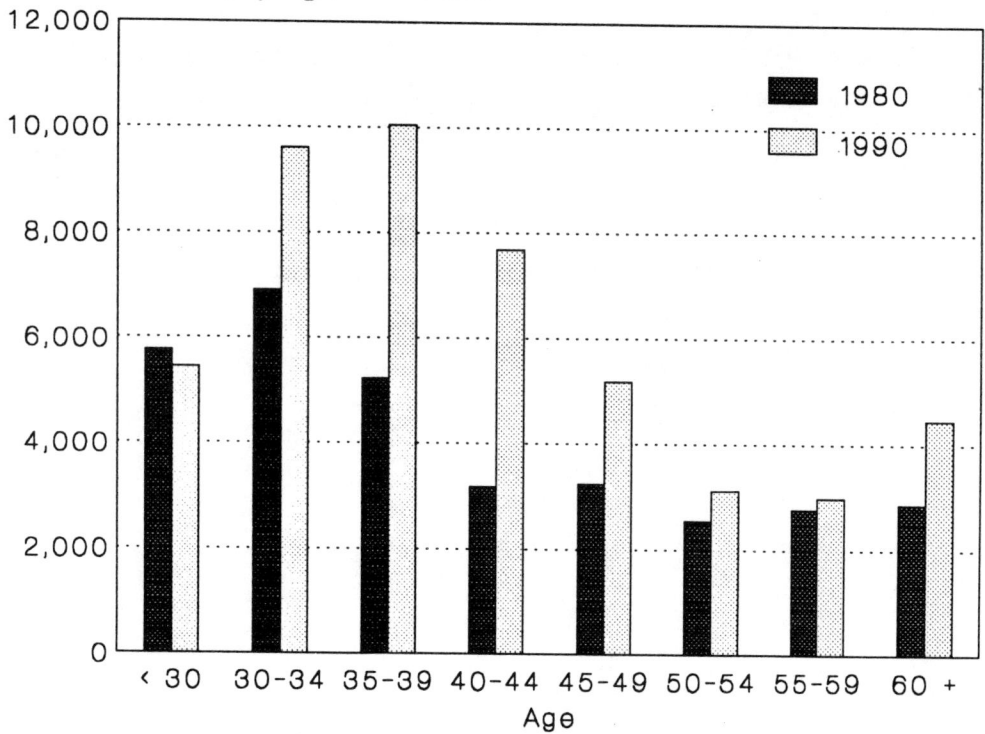

Figure 6-7. Veterinarians, by Age, 1991

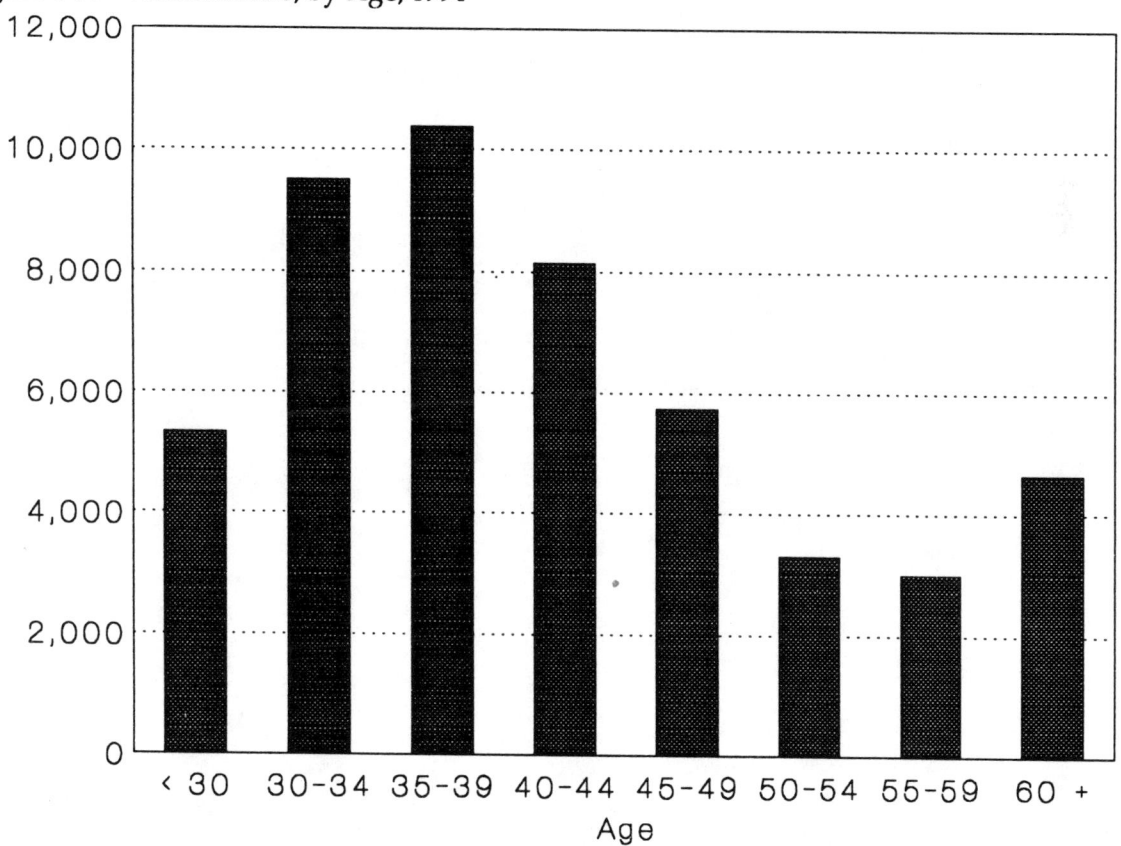

Veterinary Medical Profession

■ PRIMARY EMPLOYMENT

Veterinarians provide a wide variety of services in private clinical practice, teaching and research, government services, military service, industry, and other specialized areas.

Eighty percent of veterinarians work in private clinical practice to diagnose, control, and prevent diseases and other health problems. Veterinarians examine animal patients, immunize them against diseases, and advise owners on proper care for pets and livestock. The AVMA classifies private clinical practices as follows:

> Large Animal Exclusive: provides services for livestock and horses
> Small Animal Exclusive: provides services for companion animals (ie, dogs, cats, birds, and other small pets)
> Equine Exclusive: provides services for horses
> Mixed Animal: provides services for all types of animals, including livestock and companion animals
> Large Animal Predominant: provides services mainly for large animals, but also provides services for small animals
> Small Animal Predominant: provides services mainly for small animals, but also provides services for large animals
> Other: other private clinical practice services such as exotic, poultry, and zoological services

More than 20,000 veterinarians are in small animal exclusive practice, an increase of nearly 70% since 1980. The number of equine practitioners increased 59% over the ten-year period. Although the number of large animal exclusive practitioners increased at least 40%, the number of mixed animal and small animal predominant practitioners increased slowly (22% to 26%). The number of large animal predominant practitioners decreased between 1980 and 1990 (Table 6-4).

Table 6-4. Veterinarians, by Primary Employment, 1980, 1990, 1991

Primary Employment	1980 No.	1980 Pct.	1990 No.	1990 Pct.	1991 No.	1991 Pct.	Change 1980-1990 No.	Change 1980-1990 Pct.
Total	32,268	100.0	45,755	100.0	46,814	100.0	13,487	41.8
Private Clinical	25,499	100.0	36,828	100.0	37,615	100.0	11,329	44.4
Large Animal Exclusive	1,177	4.6	1,657	4.5	1,698	4.5	480	40.8
Large Animal Predominant	4,424	17.3	4,271	11.6	4,199	11.2	-153	-3.5
Mixed Animal	2,582	10.1	3,211	8.7	3,159	8.4	629	24.4
Small Animal Predominant	4,148	16.3	5,087	13.8	5,148	13.7	939	22.6
Small Animal Exclusive	11,724	46.0	19,921	54.1	20,614	54.8	8,197	69.9
Equine Exclusive	1,032	4.0	1,641	4.5	1,634	4.3	609	59.0
Other	412	1.6	1,040	2.8	1,163	3.1	628	152.4
Public and Corporate	6,769	100.0	8,927	100.0	9,199	100.0	2,158	31.9
College or University	2,849	42.1	4,393	49.2	4,438	48.2	1,544	54.2
Federal Government	1,133	16.7	1,137	12.7	1,201	13.1	4	0.4
State or Local Government	665	9.8	704	7.9	717	7.8	39	5.9
Uniformed Services	614	9.1	533	6.0	533	5.8	-81	-13.2
Industry	868	12.8	1,236	13.8	1,310	14.2	368	42.4
Other	640	9.5	924	10.4	1,000	10.9	284	44.4

Twenty percent of veterinarians work in public or corporate employment (Table 6-4). These employment opportunities include:

> College or University: teaching and research
> Federal, State, or Local Government: control or eliminate
>   livestock diseases, and protect the public from animal
>   diseases that can affect people
> Uniformed Services: serve as officers in the US Army
>   Veterinary Corps, biomedical research and development
>   within the military and other governmental agencies
> Industry: research, development, and management within
>   agribusiness and pharmaceutical companies
> Other: other public or corporate employment such as aquatic animal
>   medicine, space medicine, animal shelters, racetracks, ranches,
>   circuses, and zoos

The changing distribution of veterinarians, by primary employment, from 1980 to 1990 is illustrated in Figure 6-8. There is continued growth in the number of small animal veterinarians and relatively small growth or stabilization in the number of large animal veterinarians and in public-employment or corporate-employment veterinarians. Figure 6-9 shows the relative proportions of veterinarians in each primary employment type.

Veterinary Medical Profession

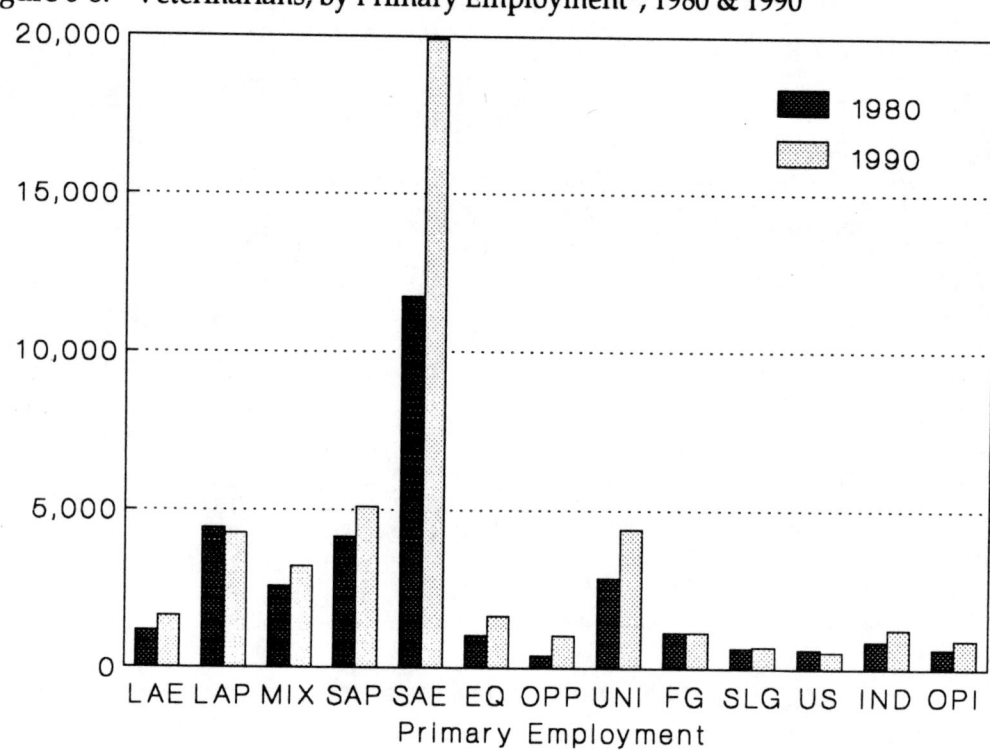

Figure 6-8. Veterinarians, by Primary Employment*, 1980 & 1990

*Employment: LAE = Large Animal Exclusive; LAP = Large Animal Predominant; MIX = Mixed Animal; SAP = Small Animal Predominant; SAE = Small Animal Exclusive; EQ = Equine Exclusive; OPP = Other Private Practice; UNI = College or University; FG = Federal Government; SLG = State or Local Government; US = Uniformed Services; IND = Industry; OPI = Other Public or Corporate

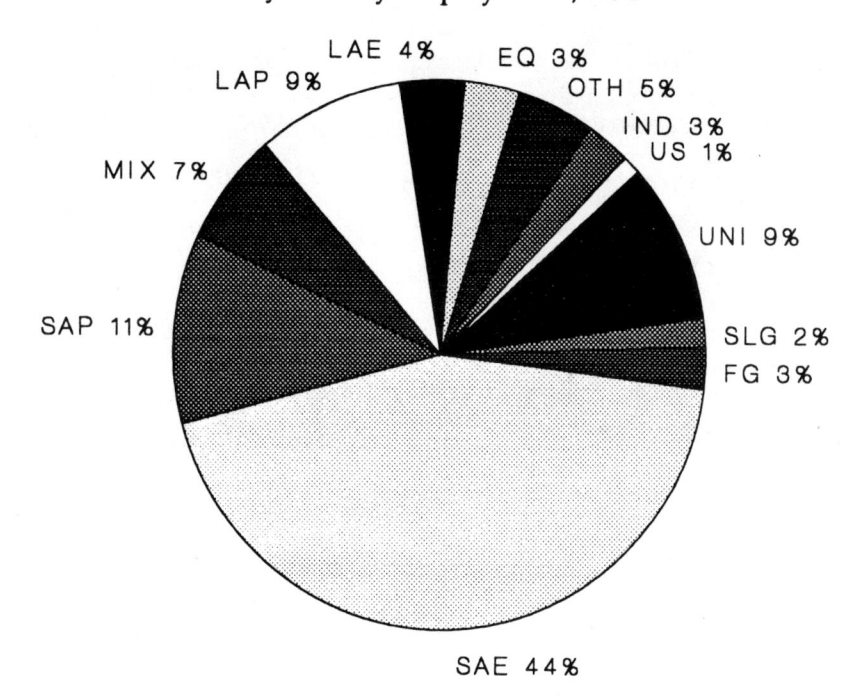

Figure 6-9. Veterinarians, by Primary Employment*, 1991

- LAE 4%
- EQ 3%
- LAP 9%
- OTH 5%
- IND 3%
- US 1%
- MIX 7%
- UNI 9%
- SAP 11%
- SLG 2%
- FG 3%
- SAE 44%

*Employment: EQ = Equine Exclusive; LAE = Large Animal Exclusive; LAP = Large Animal Predominant; MIX = Mixed Animal; SAP = Small Animal Predominant; SAE = Small Animal Exclusive; FG = Federal Government; SLG = State or Local Government; UNI = College or University; US = Uniformed Services; IND = Industry; OTH = Other Practice and Public or Corporate Combined

■ VETERINARY MEDICAL COLLEGE

To earn a veterinary medical degree, a person must generally complete at least 7 years of college education. This includes a minimum of 3 years of pre-veterinary education and 4 years in a school or college of veterinary medicine.

There are 27 AVMA-accredited colleges of veterinary medicine in the US. Each school is evaluated regularly by the AVMA and must maintain high standards of excellence in order to keep its accreditation.

The Ohio State University and Texas A&M University are estimated to have graduated the most veterinarians with 3,446 and 3,497 total graduates, respectively. Approximately 5% of veterinarians who are known to the AVMA and are active in veterinary medicine graduated from Canadian and other foreign veterinary colleges.

Figure 6-10 illustrates the estimated number of active veterinarians graduated from each of the 27 US veterinary medical colleges.

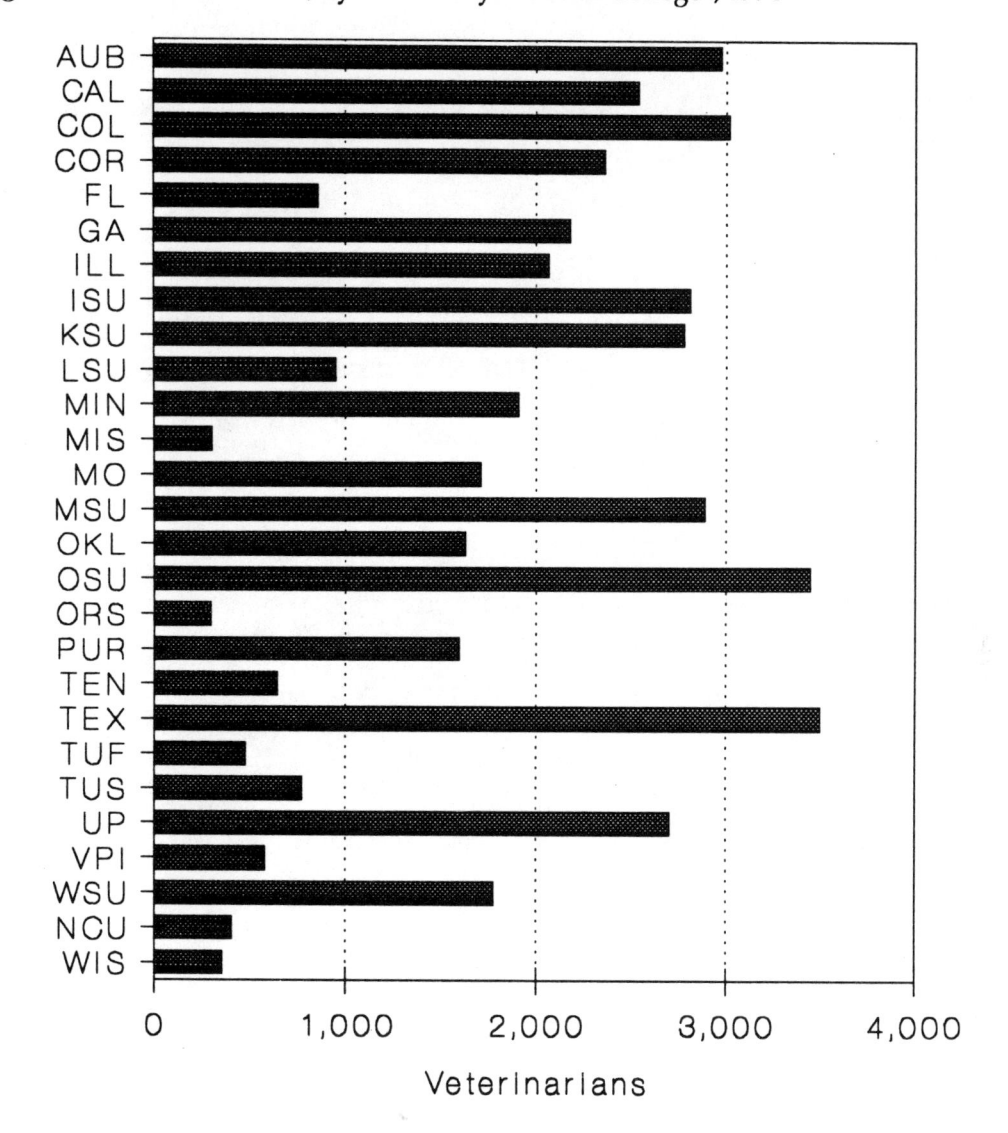

Figure 6-10. Veterinarians, by Veterinary Medical College*, 1991

*College: AUB = Auburn University; CAL = University of California; COL = Colorado State University; COR = Cornell University; FL = University of Florida; GA = University of Georgia; ILL = University of Illinois; ISU = Iowa State University; KSU = Kansas State University; LSU = Louisiana State University; MIN = University of Minnesota; MIS = Mississippi State University; MO = University of Missouri; MSU = Michigan State University; OKL = Oklahoma State University; OSU = The Ohio State University; ORS = Oregon State University; PUR = Purdue University; TEN = University of Tennessee; TEX = Texas A&M University; TUF = Tufts University; TUS = Tuskegee University; UP = University of Pennsylvania; VPI = Virginia/Maryland Regional; WSU = Washington State University; NCU = North Carolina State University; WIS = University of Wisconsin

Veterinary Medical Profession

■ YEAR OF GRADUATION

Approximately 48% of all veterinarians have graduated from veterinary medical college since 1980, 26% between 1970 and 1980, and about 15% between 1970 and 1980. Even though the number of veterinarians increased in the early 1980's, the rate of increase slowed during the late 1980's (Table 6-5).

Figure 6-11 represents the distribution of veterinarians according to year-of-graduation intervals. The increased number of veterinarians reflects the increased number of graduates over time and the number of veterinarians that remain active in veterinary medicine.

Table 6-5. Veterinarians, by Year of Graduation, 1980, 1990, 1991

Year of Graduation	1980 No.	1980 Pct.	1990 No.	1990 Pct.	1991 No.	1991 Pct.
Total	32,734	100.0	48,666	100.0	50,173	100.0
Prior to 1960	9,668	29.5	5,832	12.0	5,440	10.8
1960 - 1964	3,532	10.8	3,318	6.8	3,309	6.6
1965 - 1969	4,501	13.8	4,380	9.0	4,366	8.7
1970 - 1974	5,799	17.7	5,636	11.6	5,625	11.2
1975 - 1979	7,481	22.9	7,328	15.1	7,289	14.5
1980 - 1984	1,753	5.4	9,636	19.8	9,572	19.1
1985 - 1989	*	*	10,500	21.6	10,521	21.0
1990 - 1991	*	*	2,036	4.2	4,051	8.1

* Not applicable

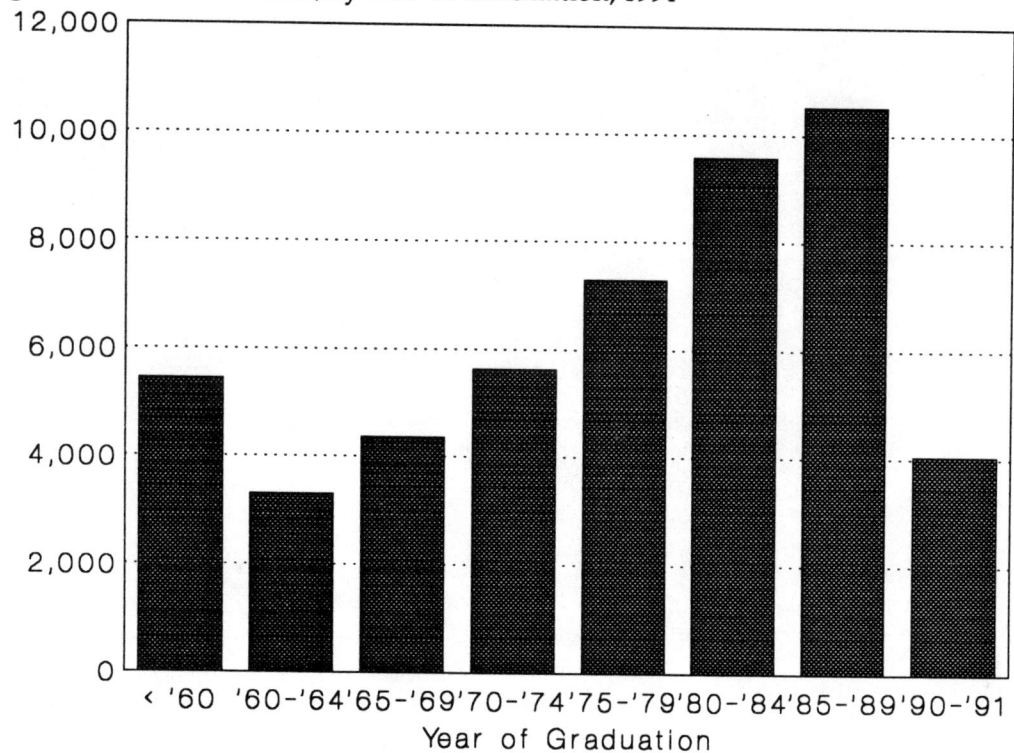

Figure 6-11. Veterinarians, by Year of Graduation, 1991

APPENDIX A

Study Methodology

■ SURVEY

In November 1991, the Center for Information Management was commissioned by the Executive Board of the American Veterinary Medical Association to conduct a nationwide study of US households to update, expand, and report information on the companion animal market.

The study was designed to enable statistical estimation of the dog and cat populations at the state level, and horse and bird populations at the regional level. A sample of 80,000 randomly selected representative households was determined to be of sufficient size to accomplish this purpose. We anticipated a 70% response rate, yielding an estimated target response sample of approximately 56,000 households for the analysis.

The survey of US households was conducted in January and February of 1992. The survey questionnaire, developed as a two-sided card, consisted of two sections.

The first section sought data on companion animal ownership during 1991, including the number of animals owned anytime during the year, the number owned at year-end, and the number of animals owned according to age of the animals. Species listed on the survey included dog, cat, bird, and horse. Two blank lines were provided for pet owners to write in two other types of pets. Also in the first section, respondents provided data on the total number of times their pet was seen by a veterinarian in 1991, total dollars spent at veterinary hospitals and clinics, total dollars spent on pet food, and the percentage of their expenditures for pet food spent at veterinary hospitals and clinics.

Appendices

In the second section, attention was focused on use of veterinary services. Companion animal owners indicated if they had a veterinarian currently and listed services or products provided during their pets' most recent veterinary visit. The questionnaire was designed to enable the respondent to answer these questions for each primary type of companion animal.

The questionnaire was mailed by NFO Research, Inc. to its consumer survey panel in two phases: first, to 30,000 households on January 15; second, to 50,000 other households on February 1, 1992. Both samples, totaling 80,000 households, were randomly selected from the NFO, Inc. national consumer research panel of 400,000 US households.

NFO's consumer household panel is developed and maintained to match, on the basis of such variables as age of household head, annual household income, and size of household, the demographic distribution of all US households according to the latest US Census demographic data.

Of the 80,000 households surveyed, 55,143 households returned usable survey questionnaires. This represented a 68.9% response rate. The respondent group was analyzed, compared with the total population of households, and determined to be a representative sample of the population.

Appendices

■ SAMPLE REPRESENTATIVENESS

The respondent group was analyzed and compared with the total population of households in regard to household characteristics, geographic distribution, market size (or population density), age of household head, annual household income, and size of household.

The distributions across family and non-family categories were nearly identical between US households and survey respondents (Table A-1). Family households represented 70.3% of respondents, compared with 70.8% of all households; non-family households represented 29.7% of respondents, compared with 29.2% of all households. Within family and non-family subgroups among respondents, there existed slight over-representation of husband-wife households, and householder living alone households. These slight deviations in household characteristics were not considered to have influenced statistical estimation procedures.

Table A-1. Sample Representativeness: Household Characteristics

Households	US Households (Percent)	Survey Respondents (Percent)
Family	70.8	70.3
Husband-wife	56.0	58.4
Male head of household, no wife	3.1	2.1
Female head of household, no husband	11.7	9.8
Non-family	29.2	29.7
Householder living alone	24.7	25.9
Householder with nonrelatives	4.5	3.8
Total	100.0	100.0

Appendices

The geographic distribution of US households and survey respondents were compared by census divisions (Table A-2). Differences between the two distributions were all within one percentage point. The respondent group was concluded to be a representative sample of the population, with respect to geographic division of the country.

Table A-2. Sample Representativeness: Geographic Division

Division	US Households (Percent)	Survey Respondents (Percent)
New England	5.4	5.5
Middle Atlantic	15.3	15.7
East North Central	17.0	17.6
West North Central	7.4	7.7
South Atlantic	18.0	17.5
East South Central	6.3	6.1
West South Central	10.5	9.8
Mountain	5.5	5.5
Pacific	14.6	14.6
Total	100.0	100.0

The respondent group also was concluded to be a representative sample of the population, with respect to population density (Table A-3).

Table A-3. Sample Representativeness: Population Density

Population	US Households (Percent)	Survey Respondents (Percent)
Under 100,000	23.3	23.9
100,000 to 499,999	15.8	16.0
500,000 to 1,999,999	20.5	20.5
2,000,000 and over	40.4	39.6
Total	100.0	100.0

Analysis of the distribution by age of the head of household showed that there existed slight over-representation among respondents of family households with a head of household more than 50 years old, and non-family households with a female head of household 35 years old or older (Table A-4). These slight deviations by age of head of household were not considered to have influenced statistical estimation procedures.

Table A-4. Sample Representativeness: Age of Head of Household

Age	US Households (Percent)	Survey Respondents (Percent)
Family		
Under 30 years	12.1	9.4
30 to 39 years	19.5	17.9
40 to 49 years	15.2	15.4
50 to 59 years	9.9	11.1
60 years and over	13.9	16.5
Non-family		
Male, under 35 years	5.1	3.8
Male, 35 years and over	7.7	7.9
Female, under 35 years	3.4	3.1
Female, 35 years and over	13.2	15.0
Total	100.0	100.0

Appendices

The distributions of all US households and of respondents were very similar, with respect to annual household income (Table A-5).

Table A-5. Sample Representativeness: Annual Household Income

Income	US Households (Percent)	Survey Respondents (Percent)
Under $12,500	18.7	18.3
$12,500 to $24,999	20.7	21.2
$25,000 to $39,999	22.4	22.5
$40,000 to $59,999	20.0	20.0
$60,000 and over	18.2	18.0
Total	100.0	100.0

Analysis by size of household showed that 1-member and 2-member households were slightly over-represented among respondents. It was concluded that for purposes of statistical estimation, the slight variations in the distributions were not important (Table A-6).

Table A-6. Sample Representativeness: Size of Household

Household Size	US Households (Percent)	Survey Respondents (Percent)
1 member	24.7	25.9
2 members	32.6	35.1
3 members	17.3	16.3
4 members	15.5	14.2
5 or more members	9.9	8.5
Total	100.0	100.0

■ STATISTICAL INFERENCE

Percentage estimates were derived from this survey and used to calculate national population estimates. The precision of the estimates is influenced by sample size, confidence coefficient and percentage result. The precision of the national estimates was very high because of the large sample of households. For example, the percentage of households that owned a dog in 1991 was 36.5%. The statistical error was only 0.4%. It may be stated, therefore, that there is a 95% probability that the interval 36.1% to 36.9% contained the true, but unknown, percentage of US households that owned dogs.

The percentage of households that owned dogs or cats was estimated for each state. Because the sample sizes in each state were less than the national sample, the statistical error associated with the estimated percentage of dog-owning households in each state increased and varied among states. The respondent sample size in California was 5,987, and the statistical error was 1.2%. In contrast, the respondent sample size for Wyoming was only 104, and the statistical error was 9.6%.

The percentage of households that owned birds or horses was estimated by census division, and not by state because of insufficient statistical confidence associated with bird and horse population estimates at the state level.

Percentage estimates at the national, regional, and state levels were based on the US Census Bureau's Series B projections of total US households. According to this projection, there were 94,700,000 US households in 1991.

APPENDIX B

Resources

American Veterinary Medical Association   (708) 925-8070
    1931 North Meacham Road, Suite 100
    Schaumburg, IL 60173-4360

Center for Information Management	Ext. 297
Public Information	Ext. 271
AVMA Foundation	Ext. 207

The American Kennel Club, Inc.   (212) 696-8288
    51 Madison Avenue
    New York, NY 10010

Cat Fanciers' Association   (908) 528-9797
    1805 Atlantic Avenue
    Manasquan, NJ 08736

FORMULAS

Most communities do not have data on the number of households owning dogs, cats, birds, and horses or on the number of these pets in their communities. The following simple formulas have been developed, using national statistics from this report, so you can estimate the number of pets and pet-owning households in your community. We are confident that these formulas will give you approximations of the number of pet-owning households or the pet population in your community, on the assumption that the demographics of your community are similar to national demographics. The formulas, because they are based on sample survey data, should not be considered 100% accurate.

In order to use the formulas on the following pages, you need to know the total number of households in your community. If you only know the number of people in your community, divide this number by 2.63 to estimate the number of households.

Example:

Your community has 20,000 households. To estimate the number of dog-owning households in your community:

.365 x Total number of households = Number of dog-owning households

.365 x 20,000 = 7,300 dog-owning households

To estimate the number of dogs in your community of 20,000 households:

.555 x Total number of households = Number of dogs
.555 x 20,000 = 11,100 dogs

AVMA Center for Information Management
1931 N Meacham Road, Suite 100, Schaumburg, IL 60173

NUMBER OF PET-OWNING HOUSEHOLDS

Pets:

Number of pet-owning = .579 x Total number of households
households

Dogs:

Number of dog-owning = .365 x Total number of households
households

Cats:

Number of cat-owning = .309 x Total number of households
households

Birds:

Number of bird-owning = .057 x Total number of households
households

Horses:

Number of horse-owning = .002 x Total number of households
households

AVMA Center for Information Management
1931 N Meacham Road, Suite 100, Schaumburg, IL 60173

NUMBER OF PETS

Dogs:

    Number of dogs   = .555 x Total number of households

Cats:

    Number of cats   = .603 x Total number of households

Birds:

    Number of birds   = .123 x Total number of households

Horses:

    Number of horses   = .051 x Total number of households

AVMA Center for Information Management
1931 N Meacham Road, Suite 100, Schaumburg, IL 60173

INDEX

Age
- birds, 18-19
- cats, 15
- dogs, 10
- horses, 22-23
- head of household, sample, 121
- pet caretakers, 79-80
- veterinarians, 106-107

American Kennel Club, 27, 125
American Veterinary Medical Association, 99, 125

Breed Registration
- cats, 32-34
- dogs, 27-31

Birds
- age, 18-19
- demographics, 47-50
- household-owning, 3-4
- number in household, 17-18
- pet food expenditures, 81
- population, 16-17
- profiles, 70-73
- veterinarian care, 91
- veterinary expenditures, 93
- veterinary services & products, 91-92
- veterinary visits, 93

Care, veterinarian, 82, 87, 91, 94, 97
Caretaker
- age, 79-80
- gender, 79-80

Cats
- age, 15
- breeds, 32-34
- demographics, 43-46
- household-owning, 3-4
- number in household, 14
- pet food expenditures, 81
- population, 11-13
- profiles, 66-69
- veterinarian care, 87
- veterinary expenditures, 90
- veterinary services & products, 87-88
- veterinary visits, 88-89

Cat Fanciers' Association, 32, 125
Colleges, veterinary medical, 112-113

Demographics
- birds, 47-50
- cats, 43-46
- dogs, 39-42
- home ownership, 38, 42, 46, 50, 54
- horses, 51-54
- income, 37, 40, 44, 48, 52
- life-stage, 35-36, 39-40, 43-44, 47-48, 51-52
- pets, 35-38
- size, 37-38, 41, 45, 49, 53

Dogs
- age, 10
- breeds, 27-31
- demographics, 39-42
- household-owning, 2-4
- number in household, 9
- pet food expenditures, 81
- population, 6-8

Center for Information Management

Index

    profiles, 62-65
    veterinarian care, 82
    veterinary expenditures, 85-86
    veterinary services & products, 82-83
    veterinary visits, 84-85

Education, profile
    Male head of household, 61
    Female head of household, 61
Employment, veterinarians, 108-111
Expenditures
    pet food, 81
    veterinary services, 85-86, 90, 93, 96, 98

Geographic division, sample, 120
Gender
    pet caretakers, 79-80
    veterinarians, 105
Graduation, year, 114-115

Home ownership
    demographics, 38, 42, 46, 50, 54
    profiles, 59, 65, 69, 73, 77
Horses
    age, 22-23
    demographics, 51-54
    household-owning, 3-5
    number in household, 21-22
    pet food expenditures, 81
    population, 20-21
    profiles, 74-77
    veterinarian care, 94
    veterinary expenditures, 96
    veterinary services & products, 94-95
    veterinary visits, 95

Household
    characteristics, sample, 119
    populations, 1-5, 24-25

Income, household
    demographics, 37, 40, 44, 48, 52
    profiles, 57, 63-64, 67, 71, 75
    sample, 122

Life-stage
    demographics, 35-36, 39-40, 43-44, 47-48, 51-52
    profiles, 55-56, 62-63, 66-67, 70-71, 74-75

Number in Households
    birds, 17-18
    cats, 14
    dogs, 9
    horses, 21-22

Other Pets
    population, 24-25
    veterinarian care, 97
    veterinary expenditures, 98
    veterinary visits, 98

Pet Care, 79
Pet Food, 81
Pets
    demographics, 35-38
    profiles, 55-61
Population
    birds, 16-17
    cats, 11-13
    density, 60
    density, sample, 120
    dogs, 6-8

Center for Information Management

Index

horses, 20-21
households, 1-5
other pets, 24-25
veterinarians, national, 99-100
veterinarians, region, 101-104
veterinarians, state, 101-102
Products, veterinary, 82-83, 87-88, 91-92, 94-95
Profiles
    birds, 70-73
    cats, 66-69
    dogs, 62-65
    female head of household education, 61
    home ownership, 59, 65, 69, 73, 77
    horses, 74-77
    income, 57, 63-64, 67, 71, 75
    life-stage, 55-56, 62-63, 66-67, 70-71, 74-75
    male head of household education, 61
    pets, 55-61
    population density, 60
    size, 57-58, 64-65, 68, 72, 76-77
    type of residence, 59

Residence, profile, 59

Sample Representativeness
    age of household head, 121
    geographic division, 120
    household characteristics, 119
    income, 122
    population density, 120
    size, 122
Services, veterinary, 82-83, 87-88, 91-92, 94-95
Size, household
    demographics, 37-38, 41, 45, 49, 53
    profiles, 57-58, 64-65, 68, 72, 76-77
    sample, 122

Statistical inference, 123
Survey methodology, 117-118

Veterinarian care
    birds, 91
    cats, 87
    dogs, 82
    horses, 94
    other pets, 97
Veterinarians
    age, 106-107
    gender, 105
    employment, 108-111
    population, national, 99-100
    population, region, 101-104
    population, state, 101-102
    veterinary medical college, 112-113
    year of graduation, 114-115
Veterinary expenditures
    birds, 93
    cats, 90
    dogs, 85-86
    horses, 96
    other pets, 98
Veterinary services & products
    birds, 91-92
    cats, 87-88
    dogs, 82-83
    horses, 94-95
Veterinary visits
    birds, 93
    cats, 88-89
    dogs, 84-85
    horses, 95
    other pets, 98

About the
Center for Information Management

The Center for Information Management of the American Veterinary Medical Association provides survey, analysis, and database management services, advises about information sources and research methods, and develops special reports on veterinary medicine and the animal health market.

The Center provides information management services, on a contractual or grant basis, for AVMA, allied organizations, veterinary product companies, foundations, and government agencies.

For more information about the Center, please call 1-800-248-2862, extension 297.

Staff of the Center for Information Management

    J. Karl Wise, Ph.D., Director
    Jih-Jing Yang, Ph.D., Research Analyst
    Deborah J. Binder, Research Assistant
    Dana C. Bucalo, Research Assistant